THEMES IN CANADIAN LITERATURE
General Editor *David Arnason*

The Immigrant Experience

Edited by
Leuba Bailey

Macmillan of Canada

ISBN 0-7705-1261-5

Themes in Canadian Literature

The Urban Experience edited by John Stevens
The Maritime Experience edited by Michael O. Nowlan
The Frontier Experience edited by Jack Hodgins
The Prairie Experience edited by Terry Angus
Isolation in Canadian Literature edited by David Arnason and
    Alice K. Hale
The Immigrant Experience edited by Leuba Bailey
Native Peoples in Canadian Literature edited by William and
    Christine Mowat
The Artist in Canadian Literature edited by Lionel Wilson
The Search for Identity edited by James Foley
The Role of Woman in Canadian Literature edited by Elizabeth
    McCullough
Canadian Humour and Satire edited by Theresa Ford

Other titles in preparation

Printed in Canada

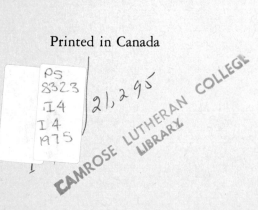

ACKNOWLEDGMENTS

Grateful acknowledgment is made for the use of copyright material.

Photographs: p. 1, Public Archives of Canada; p. 18, "The Emigrant's Welcome to Canada", Royal Ontario Museum, Toronto; p. 25, British emigrants, mid-nineteenth century, Miller Services Ltd.; p. 28, *The Telegram*, Toronto; p. 35, George Heriot: "Minuets of the Canadians", Royal Ontario Museum, Toronto; p. 36, The John Ross Robertson Collection, Toronto Public Library; p. 58, Joan Latchford; p. 60, Joan Latchford; p. 104, Joan Latchford; p. 106, Mennonites, Elmira, Ontario, Ontario Ministry of Industry and Tourism; p. 108, Information Canada Photothèque.

Margaret Atwood: "Further Arrivals" from *The Journals of Susanna Moodie* by Margaret Atwood, reprinted by permission of Oxford University Press, Canadian Branch.

A. G. Bailey: "Colonial Set" from *Border River* by A. G. Bailey, reprinted by permission of McClelland and Stewart Limited, Toronto.

Walter Bauer/Henry Beissel: "Emigrants" from *The Price of Morning*, poems by Walter Bauer translated, selected, and introduced by Henry Beissel, Prism International Press, Vancouver (1968), reprinted by permission of Henry Beissel.

Earle Birney: "Anglosaxon Street" from *Collected Poems* by Earle Birney, reprinted by permission of McClelland and Stewart Limited, Toronto.

Clark Blaise: "A Class of New Canadians", excerpts from *A North American Education* by Clark Blaise, copyright ©1973 by Clark Blaise, reprinted by permission of Doubleday & Company, Inc.

Elizabeth Brewster: "Great-Aunt Rebecca" from *Passage of Summer* by Elizabeth Brewster, reprinted by permission of McGraw-Hill Ryerson Limited.

Frances Moore Brooke: "Letter from an English Belle in Quebec", Letter XLIX from *The History of Emily Montague* by Frances Moore Brooke (1769).

Morley Callaghan: "Ancient Lineage" from *Morley Callaghan's Stories*, reprinted by permission of The Macmillan Company of Canada Limited.

Austin C. Clarke: "A Wedding in Toronto" from *When he was free and young and he used to wear silks* by Austin C. Clarke, reprinted by permission of the Author and House of Anansi Press Limited.

John Robert Colombo: "Immigrants" from *The Mackenzie Poems* (Toronto, 1965), by William Lyon Mackenzie and John Robert Colombo, reprinted by permission of the Author.

Mary Heimstra: "The Decision" adapted from *Gully Farm* by Mary Heimstra, reprinted by permission of McClelland and Stewart Limited, Toronto.

Margaret Laurence: "Christie's First Tale of Piper Gunn" from *The Diviners* by Margaret Laurence, reprinted by permission of McClelland and Stewart Limited, Toronto.

Marc Lescarbot: "A Letter from Port Royal" from *The History of New France*, Vol. III, translated by W. L. Grant, The Champlain Society, Toronto (1911).

Isabel Ecclestone Mackay: "Calgary Station", Verses 1-9, from *Complete Poems of*

Isabel Ecclestone Mackay, reprinted by permission of McClelland and Stewart Limited, Toronto.

Alexander McLachlan: "Young Canada" from *Poems and Songs* by Alexander McLachlan (1874).

Susanna Moodie: "The Fever of Immigration" adapted from *Roughing It in the Bush* by Susanna Moodie (1852).

Takeo Nakano: "My Hands" from *VOLVOX: Poetry from the Unofficial Languages of Canada . . . in English Translation*, edited by Michael Yates, Sono Nis Press (1971), reprinted by permission of Takeo Nakano.

William Paluk: "Back Door", reprinted by permission of the Author.

Al Purdy: "In the Wilderness" from *The Cariboo Horses* by Al Purdy, reprinted by permission of McClelland and Stewart Limited, Toronto.

Mordecai Richler: "Bambinger" from *The Street* by Mordecai Richler, reprinted by permission of McClelland and Stewart Limited, Toronto.

Gabrielle Roy: "The Well of Dunrea" adapted from *Street of Riches* by Gabrielle Roy, reprinted by permission of McClelland and Stewart Limited, Toronto.

F. R. Scott: " All the Spikes But the Last" from *Selected Poems* by F. R. Scott, Oxford (1966), reprinted by permission of the Author.

Allan Smith: "Metaphor and Nationality", adapted from "Metaphor and Nationality in North America" by Allan Smith, *Canadian Historial Review*, Vol. 51, No. 3, September 1970, reprinted by permission of Univerity of Toronto Press.

Joseph Stansbury: "To Cordelia" from *The Book of Canadian Poetry*, Third Edition, edited by A. J. M. Smith, Gage (1957).

Anne Wilkinson: "Summer Acres" from *The Collected Poems of Anne Wilkinson*, reprinted by permission of the Macmillan Company of Canada Limited.

CONTENTS

INTRODUCTION

We are all immigrants to Canada, even if we were born here.
                                                    Margaret Atwood

Whether ancestor or contemporary, someone connected to each of us undertook our passage to the new land. The immigrants' understanding of differences between what they left behind, and what they found here, affected them so profoundly that they spent the rest of their lives adjusting to their uprooting. For generations, in many cases, their children have had to take part in the process begun by the transplanting of a predecessor. This process can be divided into several stages, all of which are reflected in Canadian literature.

The immigrant experience begins abroad when the emigrant attempts to achieve a perspective toward his future country. How the prospective settler's mind must have soared when he was told he could own as much land as his entire present village held! He could be his own master. He could sow crops on land that was rumoured to be as fertile and virginal as the Garden of Eden. He could earn enough money to make life a paradise on earth. Nineteenth-century immigrant poets, and propagandists encouraging emigration, refer to Canada as a paradise, or "Arcadie", and modern Canadian writers still explore these comparisons.

The long, crowded voyage often tempered elation, however. The two primary realities of Canada, space and cold, made, and continue to make, a deep impression on the immigrant. The frontier at his doorstep was a threat. Without his own society surrounding and reinforcing him, he was often ill at ease. The confrontation with the new land, then, became a confrontation with the self.

The immigrant reacted to his fear by becoming either expansive or protective. He could retain his optimism and, as a kind of Adam with his Eve, inhabit paradise by forming a bond with his land. Or he could retreat to the building of a society much like the one he had left, reproducing its habits of thought and literary expression, hostile toward those who didn't belong to his group, and fearful of the howling elements that raged around his personal stockade. Immigrant writers, and writers about immigrants, frequently express in their writing a longing to be anywhere else but here.

But the exiles and aliens stayed on. They formed strong groups

1

which tried to impress on their children their own values in life—their attitudes, habits, and customs. The conflict between the point of view of the original immigrant and that of his descendants forms the basis of many works in Canadian fiction.

By learning the language, by getting ahead, or by marrying children of those who arrived in Canada earlier than they did, the "second generation" has made the attempt to integrate. Whether or not Canadian society has become fully integrated can be argued. It is often said that the structure of this country, in which the diverse parts are allowed expression, can be compared to a mosaic. As Allan Smith points out, however, this metaphor idealizes the immigrant and his experience: " . . . [The] Old World culture, when it is retained, is regarded as something to be brought out and dusted off, rather self-consciously, on special national occasions." The main thrust of *The Immigrant Experience* is to emphasize that the immigrant experience is an ongoing process in which we all participate. It is not just songs and dances and "ethnic" food. It is not poems and stories published to demonstrate local colour, or to convince Canadians that they do have an identity.

Since we cannot identify satisfactorily the sum of all these ethnic parts, Canadians are searching for identity in the initial experiences of the early immigrants to this country. We are, therefore, now participating in the final stage of the immigrant experience, the "mythologizing" of our ancestors. Their struggles and achievements have become the raw material for myth-making. A simple reference to the number of programs on television about "old-timers" and "heritages" shows that we are now imaginatively engaged in creating immigrant models, admiring their vision and vices, and, at the same time, fighting their influence on us. Many of our novels serve in this creative process, for example, Margaret Laurence's *The Stone Angel*, and Mordecai Richler's *The Apprenticeship of Duddy Kravitz*. Morley Callaghan's story, "Ancient Lineage", suggests the danger in resting at this stage for too long, pointing out that Miss Rower's pride in her family tree had "taken the place of a lover in her life". In terms of the immigrant experience, one might say that the story of Canada's family tree has taken the place of self-love in its literature.

Leuba Bailey

THE DECISION
Mary Heimstra

It was spring when we left England to go with the Barr
Colony to Canada; 31st March 1903. Daffodils were in bloom
in the gardens of the big house on Castle Hill, and there were
tall buttercups and tiny yellow-centred daisies in the small
hillside fields in front of our house. The leaves on the
hawthorn hedges and the moss on the old stone walls were a
fresh, tender green, and the ivy that covered our stone house
right to the top of the chimney-pots was thrusting out new,
inquisitive shoots. Near the pond creamy yellow cowslips were
opening, and a nightingale was looking for a nesting-place in
the big tree at the top of the lane.

There were five of us in the family then. Dad, short and
thin, with thick dark brown curls, a proud aquiline nose, a
wide forehead, and eyes that were a strange mixture of light
and shadow. They were cloud-grey edged with black, and
undershot with that deep but living shade of ocean-green that
always holds a spark. Humour was there, and understanding,
and a never-failing zest that lasted all his life.

Mother was a trim little woman even shorter than Dad. Her
eyes were big and blue, and her pink-and-white face round
and smiling. She had tiny hands and feet and a quick,
energetic way of walking that gave her tiny figure a look of
eager importance. She looked far too young to be the mother
of three children: Lily, a serious little girl with big brown eyes
and light brown curls, Jack, a baby of five months, and
myself, a big girl just past six.

The decision to leave England hadn't been either sudden or
easy. All our relatives and friends were there, and our
ancestors, who now slept under the big oaks in the old
churchyard, had walked on the narrow cobbled streets, and
lived their lives in the stone houses that stood companionably
side by side.

Dad, however, had never really liked the elbow-to-elbow
way of living, and as soon as he could he moved to the farm
on Castle Hill. There were five houses there, but they were
surrounded by fields, and we had a feeling of space. The
fields, of course, were small, and badly in need of fertilizer,

but Dad seemed content with them until the summer before Jack was born.

There were long articles about Canada in the papers that spring, and Dad began reading them, casually at first, then with deeper and deeper interest.

"Seems to be a lot of people going to Canada these days," he said one morning as he turned the pages of the *Manchester Guardian*. "It must be quite a place."

"Some people either haven't any sense, or their feet tickle." Mother looked disapprovingly at the red-and-white roast of beef she was preparing for the oven. "England's plenty good enough for me." She put the meat into a shallow roasting-pan, crossed the hearth, and shoved the pan into the dark mouth of the oven. She closed the door with a snap, and began spooning flour for a Yorkshire pudding into a yellow bowl.

"Sounds like an interesting place," Dad said after a while, and turned a page.

"What does?" Mother looked up from the pudding she was beating and smiled.

"Canada." Dad tapped the paper with a thin finger. "It says here that land there is free."

"Papers don't seem to care what they print these days." Mother dismissed them with a toss of her small, neat head. "Put some coal on the fire, will you? And give the grate a shake. There seems to be a lot of cinders in the coal lately, and they charge plenty for it, too."

"You can get wood for nothing in Canada," Dad said as he laid his paper on the table.

Mother was busy beating the pudding and didn't reply. Dad picked up the coal-scuttle, stepped over the polished brass fender that curved around the hearth, and poured a shower of coals on the open fire; then he went out to see how the new calf was getting along, but he didn't entirely forget about Canada. Scraps about it littered his conversation, and created little ripples in the even current of our lives.

While this little breeze of words, that was no stronger than

4

the wind that stirred the bluebells and carried the small white parachutes of the dandelions, eddied about us, life for me went on just as usual. I went to school, visited Grandmother and Aunt Jane in their little shop with the house attached, played hopscotch with Katie Daw, tossed stones into the Spen River, and helped make hay.

We had neither horse nor mowing-machine, and Dad said the field was so small hiring wasn't worth while, so he cut the hay with a scythe, raked it by hand, made it into hay-cocks, and left it in the field until he could hire a horse and wagon to haul it to the hayloft over the barn, or mistle as we in Yorkshire called it.

Everyone helped with the haymaking: Uncle Arthur, Dad's brother, and George Henry, a cousin who lived with us now and then. Even Mother worked for a while when she took lemonade to the sweating men. I was supposed to help, too, but I spent most of my time rolling in the sweet-smelling grass, looking for clover flowers, or sliding down the green hay-cocks when nobody was looking.

"If we had a bigger farm we could have a horse-drawn rake," Dad said one afternoon when he paused to take a deep drink of lemonade and mop his hot face and damp curly hair. "They say even the small fields in Canada are half a mile long."

"You can't believe all you hear, and only half you see," Mother said, and picked up a fork and began piling the lush hay. She wore a blue cotton dress and a big hat and looked like a morning glory.

"Some things must be true," Dad insisted. "They say the wheat grows as tall as a man."

"There's drawbacks there just as there are anywhere else," Mother said, and tried to look as if she thought Canada, and wheat as high as a man, were only fairy-tales, and not to be taken seriously; but when the man from Manitoba came she was quite worried.

He did not stay with us, he was visiting some friends in

5

Littletown, but he spent a great deal of time at Castle Hill talking to Dad. Big and loose-jointed, he looked as if he had been out in a high wind and hot sun for a long time. His red hair was always rumpled, and his eyebrows, bleached to a pinkish shade, stood on end. Red freckles spattered his face and his big ears, and his eyes looked like the pond on a cold, windy day. The backs of his broad hands were also freckle-blotched, and hair the colour of his eyebrows grew between them. While Dad milked the solemn cows he leaned against the end of the stall and talked in a flat, monotonous voice that seemed to come partly from his nose.

I paid very little attention to the man from Manitoba. His voice was harsh to my ears, but Dad's eyes brightened and his face glowed as the words unwound steadily like string from a ball.

"It sounds like a good thing," he said when the string of words paused, and he turned his head sideways and smiled while the thick white streams of milk gurgled into his bright pail.

When the milking was finished, the man from Manitoba said good night and went whistling down the tree-lined lane, and Dad, his lean face still shining, went into the house. While he washed and scalded the milk pails and had his tea, he told Mother about Canada and the advantages to be had there.

"It must be fair wonderful," he said as he sloshed scalding water into the bright pails. "The grass touches the horses' bellies, and practically everything's free. There's all the meat you can eat: deer, elk, prairie chickens, rabbits, grouse. All you have to do is shoot them. And if you want to fish you just throw a line into a lake, and the fish stun one another trying to grab your bait. You can build your own house and barn, too. It won't cost you a thing."

"There must be a catch in it somewhere," Mother said, and poured boiling water into the blue teapot. "What about the gamekeepers?"

6

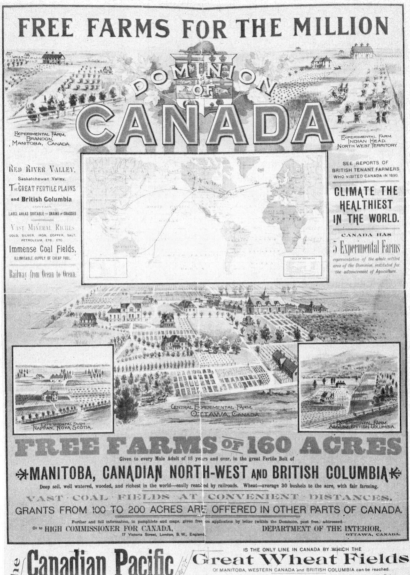

Dad said there weren't any, and no need of them. The land wasn't owned by a few as it was in England. There was a lot of vacant land, and anybody could have a piece free. "Just think on it," he said as he drew his chair to the table, his face shining, "a hundred and sixty acres, a quarter section, free. Pretty nearly twenty times more land than we have here, and not even any rent. You'd be driving your own carriage in no time, Sally."

"I don't want a carriage; horses frighten me." Mother cooled my tea by pouring it from my white mug with the brown dog on the side to the green mug with the cat on it. "I can walk to my father's and that's as far as I want to go."

"And Mary could have a horse to ride." Dad stirred his tea, and stared at the roses on the wallpaper, but he wasn't really looking at the big pink flowers, he was looking at a wide sweep of wheat on the other side of the ocean.

Mother took a slice of bread from the plate in the middle of the table and ate it slowly. "What are you going to do after tea?" she asked, not looking at Dad. "Spread manure?"

"Eh!" Dad blinked and looked confused for a moment, then he shook his head as if to clear it of a dream. "What's that?" he asked.

"That manure. I thought you were going to spread it to-night."

"Oh, ay," Dad said, and moved his feet uneasily. "I spread most of it this afternoon. I think I'll go to the club for a bit to-night. That fellow from Manitoba might come around."

"Him!" Mother pressed her lips together. "Isn't it about time he went back to where he came from?"

"He'll be gone soon." Dad got up and took his coat and cap from the hook behind the door. "I'll be back in a bit," he said, and went out. Mother tossed her neat head and got up and began clearing the table. . . .

There was a tap on the open door, and Uncle Sam came in. Mother and Uncle Sam thought a lot of each other, and no wonder. He was only fourteen months older than she was, which made them almost twins. They looked a lot alike, too, except for the sparkle. When Mother laughed her blue eyes danced, and when she walked she bounced, but Uncle Sam's feet always seemed to drag a little, and his pale eyes were always anxious even when he smiled. His straw-coloured hair was already getting thin, and his narrow shoulders looked tired.

Uncle Sam was a cabinet-maker and worked in Grandfather Gomersall's shop, but adventure had once beckoned, and he had tried to follow its enticing hand.

When he was about eighteen he had dreamed of being a soldier and going to India. He had tried again and again to enlist, but he was too thin, and although he ate a fantastic amount he couldn't gain an ounce. The army being out of the question he started to learn a trade that held out some prospects of travel, at least in England, but something happened; either the man died or the firm went out of business, and Uncle Sam came home and learned cabinet-making. He was a good workman, but the yeast had gone out of him.

Mother poked up the fire and put the kettle on for tea, and told me to go and play with my dolls for a while, which was quite all right with me. I'd expected to be put to bed.

While they waited for the kettle to boil, Mother and Uncle Sam talked. They spoke of the weather and Aunt Lily's cold, then Uncle Sam lowered his voice and said: "Sarah, I hear Walter's thinking seriously about going to Canada."

"Where did you hear that nonsense?" Mother asked.

"A fellow that goes to the club a lot told me. He said Walter talks of nothing else."

Mother laughed a little. "It won't amount to anything," she said confidently. "As soon as that man from Manitoba goes he'll forget all about Canada."

"I wish he'd go then." Uncle Sam wrinkled his pale, high forehead.

"Don't let it bother you." Mother poured boiling water into

the teapot. Uncle Sam, however, continued to worry. He said the situation was much worse than Mother thought, and he wouldn't be a bit surprised if Dad really went. Mother told him he was quite wrong, but after a while her voice lost some of its confidence, and a pleat appeared in her white forehead.

When they were on their third cup of tea Uncle Sam leaned across the table and said in an intense voice that made my ears perk: "Even if he goes, Sarah, you don't have to go with him."

"He won't go without me," Mother said, and there was happy pride in her voice, and confident grace in her shoulders.

"You never know." Uncle Sam stirred his tea. "He seems quite smitten with Canada. Be firm if he tries to persuade you, but remember, I'll help you with the bairns if he insists on going."

Mother smiled and said there was nothing to worry about, but when Uncle Sam left, the smile fell from her lips, and when I asked for a bedtime story she said there wasn't time.

TO CORDELIA
Joseph Stansbury

Believe me, Love, this vagrant life
  O'er Nova Scotia's wilds to roam,
While far from children, friends, or wife,
  Or place that I can call a home
Delights not me, — another way
My treasures, pleasures, wishes lay.

In piercing, wet, and wintry skies,
  Where man would seem in vain to toil,
I see, where'er I turn my eyes,
  Luxuriant pasture, trees, and soil.
Uncharm'd I see: — another way
My fondest hopes and wishes lay.

Oh could I through the future see
  Enough to form a settled plan,
To feed my infant train and thee
  And fill the rank and style of man:
I'd cheerful be the livelong day;
Since all my wishes point that way.

But when I see a sordid shed
  Of birchen bark, procured with care,
Design'd to shield the aged head
  Which British mercy placed there —
'Tis too, too much: I cannot stay,
But turn with streaming eyes away.

Oh! how your heart would bleed to view
  Six pretty prattlers like your own,
Expos'd to every wind that blew;
  Condemn'd in such a hut to moan.
Could this be borne, Cordelia, say?
Contented in your cottage stay.

'Tis true, that in this climate rude,
   The mind resolv'd may happy be;
And may, with toil and solitude,
   Live independent and be free.
So the lone hermit yields to slow decay:
Unfriended lives — unheeded glides away.

If so far humbled that no pride remains,
   But moot indifference which way flows the stream;
Resign'd to penury, its cares and pains;
   And hope has left you like a painted dream;
Then here, Cordelia, bend your pensive way,
And close the evening of Life's wretched day.

CHRISTIE'S FIRST TALE OF PIPER GUNN
Margaret Laurence

It was in the old days, a long time ago, after the clans was broken and battered at the battle on the moors,[1] and the dead men thrown into the long graves there, and no heather ever grew on those places, never again, for it was dark places they had become and places of mourning. Then, in those days, a darkness fell over all the lands and the crofts of Sutherland. The Bitch-Duchess[2] was living there then, and it was she who cast a darkness over the land, and sowed the darkness and reaped gold, for her heart was dark as the feathers of a raven and her heart was cold as the gold coins, and she loved no creature alive but only the gold. And her tacksmen[3] rode through the countryside, setting fire to the crofts and turning out the people from their homes which they had lived in since the beginning of all time. And it was old men and old women with thin shanks and men in their prime and women with the child inside them and a great scattering of small children, like, and all of them was driven away from the lands of their fathers and onto the wild rocks of the shore, even, to fish if they could and pry the shellfish off of the rocks there, for cod.

Well, now, the Bitch-Duchess walked her castle, there, walked and walked, and you would think God in His mercy would keep the sleep forever from her eyelids, but she slept sound enough when she had a mind to. She was not the one to

---

[1] *battle on the moors*: The "battle on the moors" was the defeat of Bonnie Prince Charlie at Culloden in April 1745. The English government used this decisive victory to extend its control into the Highlands of Scotland, by breaking up the clans and destroying the leadership of clan chiefs.

[2] *Bitch-Duchess*: Elizabeth, Countess of Sutherland, was the proprietress of the greater part of Sutherlandshire. She married George Granville, Marquess of Strafford, and in 1833 they became the Duke and Duchess of Sutherland. Together they carried out sweeping reforms of the system of land-holding. Their intention was to reduce the population of the shire and to make the land more productive for cultivation and sheep-raising. Their plan brought results which made them notorious. Hundreds of Scottish farmers, or crofters, were driven from the Highlands where they had traditionally worked the land of the Duchess's forefathers. It was these homeless people whom Lord Selkirk brought over to Canada between 1811 and 1815.

[3] *tacksman*: The tacksmen were often part of the Scottish gentry, below the great lords and above the crofters. In some cases they acted as agents of the great lords, collecting rents or helping to evict the crofters from their lands. It is interesting to note that another of the Sutherlands' reforms was to abolish the position of the tacksman.

feel shame or remorse over the people scrabbling on the rocks there like animals and like the crabs who crawl among the rocks in that place. *All the lands of Sutherland will be raising the sheep,* says the she-devil, *for they'll pay better than folk.*

Among all of them people there on the rocks, see, was a piper, and he was from the Clan Gunn, and it was many of the Gunns who lost their hearths and homes and lived wild on the stormy rocks there. And Piper Gunn, he was a great tall man, a man with the voice of drums and the heart of a child and the gall of a thousand and the strength of conviction. And when he played the pipes on the shore, there, it was the pibrochs he played, out of mourning for the people lost and the people gone and them with no place for to lay their heads except the rocks of the shore. When Piper Gunn played, the very seagulls echoed the chants of mourning, and the people wept. And Piper Gunn, he played there on the shore, all the pibrochs he knew, "Flowers of the Forest" and all them. And it would wrench the heart of any person whose heart was not dead as stone, to hear him.

Then Piper Gunn spoke to the people. *Dolts and draggards and daft loons and gutless as gutted herring you are,* he calls out in his voice like the voice of the wind from the north isles. *Why do you sit on these rocks, weeping?* says he. *For there is a ship coming,* says he, *on the wings of the morning, and I have heard tell of it, and we must gather our pots and kettles and our shawls and our young ones, and go with it into a new world across the waters.*

But the people were afraid, see? They did not dare. Better to die on the known rocks in the land of their ancestors, so some said. Others said the lands across the seas were bad lands, filled with the terrors and the demons and the beasts of the forest and those being the beasts which would devour a man as soon as look at him. *Well,* says Piper Gunn, *God rot your flabby souls then, for my woman and I will go and rear our daughters and our sons in the far land and make it ours, and you can stay here, then, and the Bitch-Duchess can have chessmen carved*

14

*from your white bones scattered here on the rocks and she shall play
her games with you in your death as she has in your life.*

Then Piper Gunn changed his music, and he played the
battle music there on the rocks. And he played "All the Blue
Bonnets Are Over the Border" and he played "Hey, Johnnie
Cope" and he played "The March of the Cameron Men" and
he played "The Gunns' Salute" which was the music of his
own clan. They say it was like the storm winds out of the
north, and like the scree and skirl of all the dead pipers who
ever lived, returned then to pipe the clans into battle.

Now Piper Gunn had a woman, and a strapping strong
woman she was, with the courage of a falcon and the beauty of
a deer and the warmth of a home and the faith of saints, and
you may know her name. Her name, it was Morag. That was
an old name, and that was the name Piper Gunn's woman
went by, and fine long black hair she had, down to her waist,
and she stood there beside her man on the rocky coast, and
watched that ship come into the harbour in that place. And
when the plank was down and the captain hailing the people
there, Piper Gunn began to walk towards that ship and his
woman Morag with him, and she with child, and he was still
playing "The Gunns' Salute".

Then what happened? What happened then, to all of them
people there homeless on the rocks? They rose and followed!
Yes, they rose, then, and they followed, for Piper Gunn's
music could put the heart into them and they would have
followed him all the way to hell or to heaven with the sound
of the pipes in their ears.

And that was how all of them came to this country, all that
bunch, and they ended up at the Red River, and that is
another story.

THE FEVER OF IMMIGRATION
Susanna Moodie

In most instances, emigration is a matter of necessity, not of
choice; and this is more especially true of the emigration of
persons of respectable connections, or of any station or position
in the world. Few educated persons, accustomed to the
refinements and luxuries of European society, ever willingly
relinquish those advantages, and place themselves beyond the
protective influence of the wise and revered institutions of
their native land, without the pressure of some urgent cause.
Emigration may, indeed, generally be regarded as an act of
severe duty, performed at the expense of personal enjoyment,
and accompanied by the sacrifice of those local attachments
which stamp the scenes amid which our childhood grew, in
imperishable characters upon the heart. Nor is it until
adversity has pressed sorely upon the proud and wounded
spirit of the well-educated sons and daughters of old but
impoverished families, that they gird up the loins of the
mind, and arm themselves with fortitude to meet and dare the
heart-breaking conflict.

The ordinary motives for the emigration of such persons
may be summed up in a few brief words; — the emigrant's
hope of bettering his condition, and of escaping from the
vulgar sarcasms too often hurled at the less wealthy by the
purse-proud, common-place people of the world. But there is
a higher motive still, which has its origin in that love of
independence which springs up spontaneously in the breasts of
the high-souled children of a glorious land. They cannot
labour in a menial capacity in the country where they were
born and educated to command. They can trace no difference
between themselves and the more fortunate individuals of a
race whose blood warms their veins, and whose name they
bear. The want of wealth alone places an impassable barrier
between them and the more favoured offspring of the same
parent stock; and they go forth to make for themselves a new
name and to find another country, to forget the past and to
live in the future. . . .

Canada's salubrious climate, its fertile soil, commercial advantages, great water privileges, its proximity to the mother country, and last, not least, its almost total exemption from taxation — that bugbear which keeps honest John Bull in a state of constant ferment — were the theme of every tongue, and lauded beyond all praise. The general interest, once excited, was industriously kept alive by pamphlets, published by interested parties, which prominently set forth all the *good* to be derived from a settlement in the Backwoods of Canada; while they carefully concealed the toil and hardship to be endured in order to secure these advantages. They told of lands yielding forty bushels to the acre, but they said nothing of the years when these lands, with the most careful cultivation, would barely return fifteen; when rust and smut, engendered by the vicinity of damp over-hanging woods, would blast the fruits of the poor emigrant's labour, and almost deprive him of bread. They talked of log houses to be raised in a single day, by the generous exertions of friends and neighbours, but they never ventured upon a picture of the disgusting scenes of riot and low debauchery exhibited during the raising, or upon a description of the dwellings when raised — dens of dirt and misery, which would, in many instances, be shamed by an English pig-sty. The necessaries of life were described as inestimably cheap; but they forgot to add that in remote bush settlements, often twenty miles from a market town, and some of them even that distance from the nearest dwelling, the necessaries of life, which would be deemed indispensable to the European, could not be procured at all, or, if obtained, could only be so by sending a man and team through a blazed forest road, — a process far too expensive for frequent repetition.

Oh, ye dealers in wild lands — ye speculators in the folly and credulity of your fellow men — what a mass of misery, and of misrepresentation productive of that misery, have ye not to answer for! You had your acres to sell, and what to you

17

were the worn-down frames and broken hearts of the infatuated purchasers? The public believed the plausible statements you made with such earnestness, and men of all grades rushed to hear your hired orators declaim upon the blessings to be obtained by the clearers of the wilderness.

Men who had been hopeless of supporting their families in comfort and independence at home, thought that they had only to come out to Canada to make their fortunes; almost even to realise the story told in the nursery, of the sheep and oxen that ran about the streets, ready roasted, and with knives and forks upon their backs. They were made to believe that if it did not actually rain gold, that precious metal could be

THE EMIGRANTS WELCOME TO CANADA

obtained, as is now stated of California and Australia, by stooping to pick it up.

The infection became general. A Canada mania pervaded the middle ranks of British society; thousands and tens of thousands, for the space of three or four years landed upon these shores. A large majority of the higher class were officers of the army and navy, with their families — a class perfectly unfitted by their previous habits and education for contending with the stern realities of emigrant life. The hand that has long held the sword, and been accustomed to receive implicit obedience from those under its control, is seldom adapted to wield the spade and guide the plough, or try its strength against the stubborn trees of the forest. Nor will such persons submit cheerfully to the saucy familiarity of servants, who, republicans in spirit, think themselves as good as their employers. Too many of these brave and honourable men were easy dupes to the designing land-speculators. Not having counted the cost, but only looked upon the bright side of the picture held up to their admiring gaze, they fell easily into the snares of their artful seducers.

To prove their zeal as colonists, they were induced to purchase large tracts of wild land in remote and unfavourable situations. This, while it impoverished and often proved the ruin of the unfortunate immigrant, possessed a double advantage to the seller. He obtained an exorbitant price for the land which he actually sold, while the residence of a respectable settler upon the spot greatly enhanced the value and price of all other lands in the neighbourhood.

It is not by such instruments as those I have just mentioned, that Providence works when it would reclaim the waste places of the earth, and make them subservient to the wants and happiness of its creatures. The Great Father of the souls and bodies of men knows the arm which wholesome labour from infancy has made strong, the nerves which have become iron by patient endurance, by exposure to weather, coarse fare, and rude shelter; and He chooses such, to send forth into the forest to hew out the rough paths for the advance of civilization. These men become wealthy and prosperous, and form the bones and sinews of a great and rising country. Their labour is wealth, not exhaustion; it produces independence and content, not home-sickness and despair. What the Backwoods of Canada are to the industrious and ever-to-be-honoured sons of honest poverty, and what they are to the refined and accomplished gentleman, these simple sketches will endeavour to portray. They are drawn principally from my own experience, during a sojourn of nineteen years in the colony.

IMMIGRANTS

Found by John Robert Colombo

Quebec,
April 22nd to 25th,
1831.
One forenoon
I went on board the ship
Airthy Castle,
from Bristol,
immediately after her arrival.
The passengers were in number 254,
all in the hold or steerage;
all English, from about Bristol,
Bath, Frome, Warminster, Maiden Bradley, &c.
I went below,
and truly it was a curious sight.
About 200 human beings,
male and female,
young, old, and middle-aged;
talking, singing, laughing, crying, eating, drinking,
     shaving, washing;
some naked in bed, and others dressing to go
     ashore;
handsome young women (perhaps some)
and ugly old men,
married and single;
religious and irreligious.
Here a grave matron
chaunting selections
from the latest edition
of the last new hymn book;
there, a brawny plough-boy
"pouring forth the sweet melody
of Robin Adair".
These settlers were poor,
but in general
they were fine-looking people,

and such as I was glad
to see come to America.
They had had a fine passage
of about a month,
and they told me
that no more ship loads of settlers
would come from the same quarter
this year.
I found that it was
the intention of many of them
to come to Upper Canada.
Fortune may smile on some,
and frown on others;
but it is my opinion
that few among them will forget
being cooped up below deck
for four weeks
in a moveable bedroom,
with 250 such fellow-lodgers
as I have endeavoured to describe.

William Lyon Mackenzie

EMIGRANTS
Walter Bauer

They came from San Cataldo,
from Racalmuto, Villa San Giovanni,
they had escaped from Sicily's African sun
and from perpetual poverty.
They sat on deck the "Argentina"
as if by the well in their village and chatted
as though there were no ocean
nor, after their arrival,
all those speechless things
like the Atlantic even colder than this.
The boat was for them a slowly moving
San Cataldo or wherever it was they came from
with their beggarly boxes.
Looking into their eyes you could see
tremendous kinds of hope:
Studebaker or Buick,
refrigerator, radio, a house,
and enough to eat always.
Some of the young men walked
with a sway of the hip
as if they had conquered Montreal (which none of them knew)
or all the gold-mines of the north.
And like a messianic pronouncement
one word was heard again and again:
money.

Translated from the German
by Henry Beissel

FURTHER ARRIVALS
Margaret Atwood

After we had crossed the long illness
that was the ocean, we sailed up-river

On the first island
the immigrants threw off their clothes
and danced like sandflies

We left behind one by one
the cities rotting with cholera,
one by one our civilized
distinctions

and entered a large darkness.

It was our own
ignorance we entered.

I have not come out yet

My brain gropes nervous
tentacles in the night, sends out
fears hairy as bears,
demands lamps; or waiting

for my shadowy husband, hears
malice in the trees' whispers.

I need wolf's eyes to see
the truth.

I refuse to look in a mirror.

Whether the wilderness is
real or not
depends on who lives there.

From Margaret Atwood's book of poems, *The Journals of Susanna Moodie*, inspired by Mrs.
Moodie's experiences as a pioneer.

CALGARY STATION

Isabel Ecclestone Mackay

Dazzled by sun and drugged by space they wait,
These homeless peoples, at our prairie gate;
Dumb with the awe of those whom fate has hurled,
Breathless, upon the threshold of a world!

From near-horizoned, little lands they come,
From barren country-side and deathly slum,
From bleakest wastes, from lands of aching drouth,
From grape-hung valleys of the smiling South,
From chains and prisons, ay, from horrid fear,
(Mark you the furtive eye, the listening ear!)
And all amazed and silent, scared and shy —
An alien group beneath an alien sky!

See — on that bench beside the busy door —
There sleeps a Roman born: upon the floor
His wife, dark-haired and handsome, takes her rest,
Their black-eyed baby tugging at her breast.
Her hands lie still. Her brooding glances roam
Above the pushing crowd to her far home,
And slow she smiles to think how fine 'twill be
When they (so rich!) return to Italy.

Yonder, with stolid face and tragic eye,
Sits a lone Russian; as we pass him by
He neither stirs nor looks; his inner gaze
Sees not the future fair, but, troubled, strays
To the dark land he left but can't forget,
Whose bonds, though broken, hold him prisoner yet.

Here is a Pole — a worker; though so slim
His muscle is of steel — no fear for him;
He is the breed which conquers; he is nerved
To fight and fight again. Too long he served,
Man of a subject race! His fierce, blue eye

Roams like a homing eagle o'er the sky,
So limitless, so deep! for such as he
Life has no higher bliss than to be free.

This little Englishman with jaunty air
And tweed cap perched awry on close-trimmed hair —
He, with his faded wife and noisy band,
Has come from Home to seek a promised land —
He feels himself aggrieved, for no one said
That things would be so big and so — outspread!
He thinks of London with a pang of grief;
His wife is sobbing in her handkerchief.
But all his children stare with eager eyes.
This is their land. Already they surmise
Their heritage, their chance to live and grow,
Won for them by their fathers, long ago!

Another generation, and this Scot,
Whose longing for the hills is ne'er forgot
Shall rear a son whose eye will never be
Dim with a craving for that distant sea,
Those barren rocks, that heather's purple glow —
The ache, the burn that only exiles know!

This Irishman, who, when he sees the Green,
Turns that his shaking lips may not be seen,
He, too, shall bear a son who, blythe and gay,
Sings the old songs but in a cheerier way!
Who has the love, without the anguish sharp,
For Erin dreamingly by her golden harp!

All these and many others, patient, wait
Before our ever-open prairie gate
And, filing through with laughter or with tears,
Take what their hands can glean of fruitful years.

Here some find home who knew not home before;
Here some seek peace and some wage glorious war.
Here some who lived in night see morning dawn
And some drop out and let the rest go on.
And of them all the years take toll; they pass
As shadows flit above the prairie grass.

MY HANDS
Takeo Nakano

My hands tremble
As I sign my naturalization papers
Making me a Canadian citizen
And Canada my final resting place.

"26. No immigrant shall be permitted to land in Canada, who is feeble-minded, an idiot, or an epileptic, or who is insane, or who has had an attack of insanity within five years; nor shall any immigrant be so landed who is deaf and dumb, blind or infirm, unless he belongs to a family accompanying him or already in Canada, and which gives security, satisfactory to the Minister, and in conformity with the regulations in that behalf, if any, for his permanent support if admitted into Canada.

"27. No immigrant shall be permitted to land in Canada who is afflicted with a loathsome disease, or with a disease which is contagious or infectious, and which may become dangerous to the public health or widely disseminated, whether such immigrant intends to settle in Canada or only to pass through Canada to settle in some other country; provided that if such disease is one which is curable within a reasonably short time, the immigrant suffering therefrom may, subject to the regulations in that behalf, if any, be permitted to remain on board where hospital facilities do not exist on shore, or to leave the vessel for medical treatment, under such regulations as may be made by the Minister.

"28. No person shall be permitted to land in Canada who is a pauper, or destitute, a professional beggar, or vagrant, or who is likely to become a public charge; and any person landed in Canada who, within two years thereafter, has become a charge upon the public funds, whether municipal, provincial, or federal, or an inmate . . ."   *(from Canada's original Immigration Act)*

A LETTER FROM PORT ROYAL

Marc Lescarbot

From Port Royal,
on the Rivière de l'Equille, in
New France.
22nd August 1606.

You know well how for a long time I have had my mind and
my desire turned toward this country. By the Grace of God I
have reached it, after the trials of the ocean. These were
greater on the French side of the Bank than on this side, by
reason of the storms which are more frequent there, especially
in the neighbourhood of the Azores. We had few favouring
winds, being almost always driven northward or southward
instead of westward, whereby we were kept at sea for a full
two months and a half before setting foot on land, save at the
harbour called Port Mouton, where we went in a long-boat in
search of fresh water. The shores were sandy, and yet we found
there great quantity of peas, gooseberries, musk-roses,
walnuts, ferns, pines, cypresses, oaks, and raspberries, and also
purples, angelica, scammony, and other simples, which we
had no time to identify, since we remained there only two
hours. Thence we rounded Cape Sable, which is not the same
as Sable Island, which is three and a half degrees distant; and
at last came to anchor off the entrance to Port Royal on the
Rivière de l'Equille, where we are, the wind not being
favourable to enter. This entrance is twelve, fifteen, and
twenty fathoms deep, but sometimes it is difficult owing to its
narrowness. I call it narrow, yet it is fairly wide, about the
same as from the Cross of the Carmelites to the
Strappado-gibbet of the Place Maubert, and with a mountain
on either hand. There are eddies which sometimes make this
entrance difficult if the wind is not from the right quarter.

This harbour is the most beautiful spot that can be
imagined in all the world, being eight leagues in
circumference, and surrounded on all sides with most
delightful slopes. I have composed some verses about it which

M. de Reguesson, or in his absence M. de Vaudin, will show you, with the letter which I have written him at greater length than this. The sea here on this side of the Bank so abounds in fish that one never casts a line in vain, which is one of the true perfections of life; for there we leave off meat for fish, so good is it, and one must give this sea the credit for part of the sustenance of the whole of Christendom, which is caught here everywhere where one can throw a line; for our sailors fished successfully in fifty and sixty fathoms, and at twenty, thirty, and forty fathoms one never fails to get a bite, though of course some spots yield more than others. After reaching the Bank, we had the feeling of being at home, as indeed we were: and all comers from the Old World must salute the King's ship.

M. de Poutrincourt has had a field dug over, wherein he has sown seeds of all sorts with the intention of doing the same in a fortnight and again in a month; in short, at every season to make trial of the soil. In a week the seeds have already sprouted well above the ground. Some time ago the savages left lying about some grains of wheat, oats, peas, and beans, which had been given them, and although these had fallen accidentally and on untilled soil, yet they have grown most successfully, and the grains are goodly and ready for grinding, as we saw for ourselves at the spot where the savages' encampment stood.

We intended going on farther without landing, but those who had been left here having lost their long-boat in their voyage of discovery along the coast, we were unable to proceed farther. Yet I think that we shall do so with the ship which brought us here; one on the one hand to France, and the other will make this exploration of the coast as far as 40° or 38°.

There are two reasons for changing our abode, apart from reasons of state: first, the scurvy; secondly, the laziness of the savages in these parts, who are not accustomed to work, whereas those who live sixty and eighty leagues farther on till the soil, and dig it up lightly, so that they reap from it millet and Indian corn such as I have sometimes seen in France. The land is open; there are more meadows than here and also wild vines in abundance. I have been told that they are also found in some places about here. In any case, that country being on the forty-fifth parallel is full of fair slopes and very suitable for vines. There are also squashes and walnut trees, of which I have seen the fruit. They wish to make me believe that that country is a thousand times fairer than this; but I do not believe a word of it, for the Earthly Paradise could not be more delightful than these regions. As for the scurvy, the true and certain remedy in my opinion is to burn down the woods and thus to purify the soil, which is full of rotten wood which has fallen there since the beginning of time. The vapours from this are sucked up by the sun and make the air unhealthy. This would also cure another evil, which is the insatiability of certain small red flies, with long feet, which come out of the woods, from which it is hard to protect oneself when there is no wind, unless the heat is great, for this they cannot endure, nor wind or cold. Moreover, a special property which protects the country is that the sea in summer is almost always driven back from the land; and besides, the land is in itself difficult of approach by ships, by reason of the multitude of islands which fringe it; and once at least we had a narrow escape when we found ourselves almost among the breakers, and would have fallen among them had it not been for a sudden burst of sunlight which God sent us, which disappeared forthwith. But I become too prolix and fear to prejudice your clients by my interruptions.

LETTER FROM AN ENGLISH BELLE IN QUEBEC
Frances Moore Brooke

Letter to Miss Rivers, Clarges Street

Silleri, January 1

It is with difficulty I breathe, my dear; the cold is so amazingly intense as almost totally to stop respiration. I have business, the business of pleasure, at Quebec; but have not courage to stir from the stove.

We have had five days, the severity of which none of the natives remember to have ever been equaled: 'tis said, the cold is beyond all the thermometers here, tho' intended for the climate.

The strongest wine freezes in a room which has a stove in it; even brandy is thickened to the consistence of oil: the largest wood fire, in a wide chimney, does not throw out its heat a quarter of a yard.

I must venture to Quebec to-morrow, or have company at home: amusements are here necessary to life; we must be jovial, or the blood will freeze in our veins.

I no longer wonder the elegant arts are unknown here; the rigour of the climate suspends the very powers of the understanding; what then must become of those of the imagination? Those who expect to see
"A new Athens rising near the pole",
will find themselves extremely disappointed. Genius will never mount high, where the faculties of the mind are benumbed half the year.

'Tis sufficient employment for the most lively spirit here to contrive how to preserve an existence, of which there are moments that one is hardly conscious: the cold really sometimes brings on a sort of stupefaction.

We had a million of beaux here yesterday, notwithstanding the severe cold: 'tis the Canadian custom, calculated I suppose for the climate, to visit all the ladies on New-year's-day, who sit dressed in form to be kissed: I assure you, however, our kisses could not warm them; but we were obliged, to our eternal disgrace, to call in raspberry brandy as an auxiliary.

You would have died to see the men; they look just like so many bears in their open carrioles, all wrapped in furs from head to foot; you see nothing of the human form appear, but the tip of a nose.

They have intire coats of beaver skin exactly like Friday's in Robinson Crusoe, and casques on their heads like the old knights errant in romance; you never saw such tremendous figures; but without this kind of cloathing it would be impossible to stir out at present.

The ladies are equally covered up, tho' in a less unbecoming style; they have long cloth cloaks with loose hoods, like those worn by the market-women in the north of England. I have one in scarlet, the hood lined with sable, the prettiest ever seen here, in which I assure you I look amazingly handsome; the men think so, and call me the *Little red riding-hood*; a name which becomes me as well as the hood.

The Canadian ladies wear these cloaks in India silk in summer, which, fluttering in the wind, look really graceful on a fine woman.

Besides our riding-hoods, when we go out, we have a large buffaloe's skin under our feet, which turns up, and wraps round us almost to our shoulders; so that, upon the whole, we are pretty well guarded from the weather as well as the men.

Our covered carrioles too have not only canvas windows (we dare not have glass, because we often overturn), but cloth curtains to draw all round us; the extreme swiftness of these carriages also, which dart along like lightening, helps to keep one warm, by promoting the circulation of the blood. . . .

I suppose Pygmalion's statue was some frozen Canadian gentlewoman, and a sudden warm day thawed her. I love to expound ancient fables, and I think no exposition can be more natural than this.

Would you know what makes me chatter so this morning?

Papa has made me take some excellent *liqueur*; 'tis the mode here; all the Canadian ladies take a little, which makes them so *coquet* and *agréable*. Certainly brandy makes a woman talk like an angel. Adieu!

Yours,
A. Fermor.

COLONIAL SET
A. G. Bailey

That wolf, shivering by the palisade,
nosed the footprints of a hard winter,
grew thin.
The Indians are fighting drunk.
The Frenchmen keep the squaws.
"How I long to be
in Normandy.
The carriages are waiting at the door.
The ladies lie in laces at the fête,
Festin à tout manger
to gobble up
the choicest viands of the *cuisinier*,"
the water murmured,
beating its breasts shapelessly on the shore.

A cold agony kept pace with the storm,
keeping the temper of the waves leashed,
towering with destination in the northeast,
beating away warm
blood from the heart's core,
checking the arteries,
clogging the burden of the veins,
congealing stagnant lusts in an inland pool.
Animalculae shrivel and die in their sacks.
The beaver cowers in his dam. The caribou
snorts frostily.
Hoofs clatter on the ice-pack.
The rampikes of the forest
attain a brittle silence.

YOUNG CANADA, or JACK'S AS GOOD AS HIS MASTER

Alexander McLachlan

I love this land of forest grand!
    The land where labour's free;
Let others roam away from home,
    Be this the land for me!
Where no one moils, and strains and toils,
    That snobs may thrive the faster;
And all are free, as men should be,
    And Jack's as good's his master!

Where none are slaves, that lordly knaves
    May idle all the year;
For rank and caste are of the past,—
    They'll never flourish here!
And Jew or Turk if he'll but work,
    Need never fear disaster;
He reaps the crop he sowed in hope,
    For Jack's as good's his master.

Our aristocracy of toil
    Have made us what you see —
The nobles of the forge and soil,
    With ne'er a pedigree!
It makes one feel himself a man,
    His very blood leaps faster,
Where wit or worth's preferred to birth,
    And Jack's as good's his master!

Here's to the land of forests grand!
    The land where labour's free;
Let others roam away from home,
    Be this the land for me!
For here 'tis plain, the heart and brain,
    The very soul grows vaster!
Where men are free, as they should be,
    And Jack's as good's his master!

THE WELL OF DUNREA
Gabrielle Roy

At the time in question, Papa was especially well pleased with
the colony of White Russians or Ruthenians established at
Dunrea. For a reason unknown to us he called them his "Little
Ruthenians". Of all the groups he had settled, this one
prospered best. It had not yet been established for a full
decade; a short enough time in which to build a happy
settlement out of a handful of suspicious and illiterate
immigrants, let alone clear the land, build houses, and even
make God feel at home with icons and votive candles. Yet all
this and much more had the Little Ruthenians accomplished.
They were not a people absorbed in vexations, like the
Dukhobors. Agnès seemed to remember that they, likewise,
were Slavs, probably from Bucovina. Certainly the past
counted for something in their lives — a past deeply wretched
— but it was in the future, a wonderful and well-founded
future, that the little Ruthenians above all had faith when
they came to Canada. And that was the sort of settler Papa
liked: people facing forward, and not everlastingly whining
over what they had had to leave behind.

Agnès told us that Papa had described his Dunrea
settlement as a sort of paradise, and that was precisely the
word he used — a paradise. . . .

One day he had chanced to miss his way in the course of his
rounds and had stumbled on the dried-up bed of this river;
polished pebbles along its bottom and the placement of a few
trees showed that here there had been water. And Papa fell in
love with this nook of ground, once grassy and certainly
charming, which with little care would recapture its former
loveliness. He promised himself to settle some hard-working
colonists here, good colonists, intelligent enough to glimpse
what they could make of it with patience and a little
imagination. Now the Little Ruthenians, when he brought
them and showed them the bed of the Lost River, grasped at
once what Papa liked about it, what he so clearly saw; they
decided to remain there. And when Papa urged them to plant

many trees near the Lost River, so as to hold the dampness in the soil, his Little Ruthenians had followed his suggestion. Thus, from year to year the river yielded more water, and in places reached a depth of six feet. Thereafter, of their own accord, all sorts of other little trees began to grow along its shores and interlaced their branches and created a kind of tunnel of verdure through which flowed and sang the Lost River. For, even when rediscovered, it continued to be called the Lost River.

And it seems Papa told Agnès that what he liked best for his settlements was water. In that Saskatchewan, so lacking moisture, the resurrection of a river was a major business. "Fire," he had said, "and drought are my settlers' worst enemies; running water their greatest friend."

The Little Ruthenians, having placed their confidence in Papa's prediction that water would return here, had built their houses along the dry stream bed, to such good effect that ten years later, all their houses lay within the soft and murmurous protection of the trees and the water.

Papa, when he clambered out of his wagonette and hitched his mare Dolly to the edge of the well of Dunrea, beheld a ravishing landscape: scattered in the greenery lay a score of half-hidden little white houses with thatched roofs; there were as many outbuildings, equally clean, whitewashed every spring; and besides all this, beehives, dovecots, lean-tos of leaves and branches where in the heat of day the cows came for shelter; throughout the village there wandered freely flocks of white geese which filled it with their amusing clatter. And yet, Papa said, the houses were not really white; you realized that their gleaming color was softened by an extremely delicate tint, almost indiscernible, and due to the Ruthenian women's covering their walls with a thin lime wash to which they had added a dose of bluing. In the windows, which were small and low, they had red geraniums in pots. And Papa said that after having jogged for miles through a dismal countryside of stiff

grass and wild vegetation, nothing could be more attractive —
yet more surprising, too — than Dunrea. Each time he saw it,
he had to rub his eyes before he could credit them and thank
God.

Maybe, also, when he set foot in Dunrea, Papa felt the
great joy of having been right on that day when the future of
this small corner of earth had revealed itself to him; and
maybe his joy sprang even more from the fact that his Little
Ruthenians had so well fulfilled his dream.

The moment he stepped down from his rig, Papa found
himself surrounded with children; he patted their cheeks,
tweaked their ears . . . a strange thing, for with his own
children Papa never did such things. Yet perhaps those
children, more than we, had confidence in Papa; after all, we
often enough saw how tired and disappointed Papa looked; we
knew he did not always succeed in his efforts; whereas these
people believed him endowed with an almost supernatural
power. Who can ever know what peace of mind, what
certitude Papa felt among his Little Ruthenians? Isolated, far
from any other village, not yet even speaking their neighbors'
language, they must have relied wholly upon Papa, and the
trust between them was total.

The geese, the hens, the young turkeys scattered in front of
him as Papa walked along through the mass of flowers. He
always said that when settlers planted flowers, it was a sure
sign of success, of happiness. And among his Little
Ruthenians, sweet peas clambered on the fences, rows of tall
sunflowers slowly turned their enormous faces, pale poppies
spilled their smooth petals to be scattered by the wind. The
women even set out flowers along the paths that led from the
houses to the little privies; and it seems that Papa had laughed
at this excess of adornment.

Papa, however, was a serious man, and his first concern was
to look after the crops. Now for miles around the village it
was always uniformly beautiful; the lands of the Little
Ruthenians were free of weeds and well tilled; wheat, the

various grains, alfalfa, lucerne, clover — all did splendidly. In their methods, too, the little Ruthenians had followed Papa's ideas: he had advised them not to overburden the soil by trying for continuous heavy crops, but to rotate, to be patient, and they had heeded him. And maybe that is why he called his Dunrea settlement paradise. Was he not obeyed there as God had once been in His Eden? He was confident and had never yet been mistaken in all the things he had ordained for his Little Ruthenians. Yet these Little Ruthenians, Agnès elaborated, were not at all small; on the contrary, they were almost all of average stature, some of them even very tall and sturdy. Papa called them the Little Ruthenians for a reason unconnected with their size, but Agnès could not remember precisely what it was. Though, said she, it seems that in their intensely blue eyes there lingered something of childhood.

Papa made the rounds of the kitchen gardens, for he was interested in the rare vegetables the women raised there; there were garlic, cabbages, and turnips, as in all such gardens, but also dill, very large, succulent black beans, cucumbers, Papa said, as sweet as nuts, and a great many other things — melons, for instance; the Little Ruthenians were very fond of melons. Papa went here and there surrounded by an activity which hummed from every direction and yet remained invisible. He would go into one house, then another. On each threshold, the women came to kiss his hand, but Papa pulled it back; he was embarrassed by this gesture of submission. Followed by his interpreter, then, he was among his own. "For I forgot to explain," Agnès added, "Papa had had time only to learn a score or so of words in their dialect, and their English was not much better. Despite this, how well they understood each other! How they trusted the interpreter when he said: 'The gentleman sent by the government informs you that such and such measures should be taken . . . ' or else, 'Boris Masaliuk respectfully inquires whether. . .' "

Then the meal was ready. While the men talked business, the women had prepared the food in so great a silence that, each time, Papa was startled to hear soft words spoken near his ear: "If you please, Mr. Government, do us the great honor of coming to our table. . . ."

The men sat down; not the women, whose role now was to remain standing behind hosts and guests, attentive to pass them the various dishes. Was Papa sorry for them, was he fond of them, these silent, shy women, who hid their lovely tresses beneath kerchiefs and murmured, as they served the men, "If you please . . . "?

He had told Agnès that Ruthenian women's voices were the same as a murmuring of water and of silence. It is certain, though, that he would have preferred to see them seated at the same time as the men at their own table. This was the only fault he found with his Little Ruthenians — that they were absolute masters in their own families. Several times he was tempted to speak to them about this, to invite the women also to sit down at table . . . but he was not entirely at home.

Papa often spent a night at Dunrea. There he slept like a child. The women's voices were never high or screeching. They seemed happy. "But what does that prove?" Papa wondered. "The slaves of other days were certainly happier than their masters. Contentment is not necessarily the servant of justice." So the lot of the women at Dunrea was the only thing that upset him. He listened to them humming their babies to sleep . . . and soon he himself slipped into slumber as into a whole and deep submission. When he awoke, it was to the good smell of strong coffee which the women were preparing for him downstairs.

All that was too beautiful to last, my father would have said. How did it happen that here alone peace and plenty reigned? Everywhere else his settlers encountered obstacles. Look how it was with his Dukhobors! Among them the Devil's malice borrowed the very teaching of Christ the better to sow confusion. Indeed, in their effort always to act as Christ would have done in our epoch, to fathom the meaning of His acts, of His parables, the Dukhobors committed folly after folly. Had they not decided, on the eve of winter, to set free all their domestic animals, because, said they, "Did not our God create all creatures free, beasts as well as men?" . . .

And Papa himself began to wonder why God seemed to love the Little Ruthenians better than others. He was careful not to confuse their simple, naïve minds; he did not too severely try their good will. And from then on Papa felt a kind of anxiety. He blamed himself for having certainly been too proud of Dunrea.

Whenever influential government people, top men from the Ministry of Colonization, asked to visit settlements, Papa always took them to Dunrea. And Dunrea helped his career, earned him consideration. The railroad companies sent photographers to make pictures of the Lost River; and the Canadian Pacific Railway produced a large number of Dunrea photos, sending them to places all over the world, to Poland, to Romania, to attract immigrants. For the C.P.R. made a great deal of money from the transportation of immigrants. My father one day met a poor Czech who confided to him that he had come to Canada only because he had seen a very tempting poster: a river, golden wheat, houses "just like those at home . . . " and now this Czech was working in a mine. . . . At Dunrea, despite Papa's fears, the wheat continued to grow, the fine cattle to multiply. And since they prospered, the Little Ruthenians believed themselves better and better loved by God. They thanked Him for rains that came when they were needed, for sunshine in due season. They had no least expectation that God's gentle hand would ever weigh heavily upon them.

The Little Ruthenians had always been very careful of fire; when, from time to time, they had to burn stumps or weeds, they waited for a very calm day; and once the fire had done its work, they put it out by scattering the coals and then covering them with moist earth. Moreover, in their ever-damp oasis, within earshot of the murmuring Lost River, how could they truly have feared fire?

Now that particular summer was burning dry. Even in the Lost River the water level went down several feet. And a fire started, probably ignited by nothing more than the sun, twenty miles north of Dunrea. At first the wind drove it in another direction. My father was camping eighteen miles farther on, in a region he was looking over with a party of surveyors. During the night he awoke. The wind had changed. It was stronger and laden with an acrid smoke which hurt eyes and throat. A little later a messenger arrived on horseback. He said the fire was moving toward Dunrea. My father jumped into the wagonette; he made no attempt to follow the road, which was far from straight in that part of the country; as much as possible he took short cuts through the brambles and small, dried-up swamps. Dolly obeyed him faithfully, even though she was wounded by the sharp points of the briars. Behind him, as he crossed these gloomy stretches of scrub, my father saw the fire following him from afar, and he heard its rumble. He prayed for the Lost River. He hoped for another change in the wind, which would sweep the fire elsewhere, no matter in what direction save toward Dunrea. This sort of prayer, he admitted, was perhaps not a good prayer. Indeed, why pray for his Ruthenians rather than for the poor, lonely farms along the Lost River road? Is the misfortune that strikes those one loves greater, my father asked himself, than that which strikes those unknown to us?

Arriving at Dunrea, he ordered the men to take their horses and plows and quickly to turn under a wide belt around the village. He set other men to digging ditches. The sky had become bright red . . . and that helped along the work, since one could see by it as though it were broad daylight. But how strange a daylight! What a dreadful glow silhouetted the terrified animals, the running men, each gesture and attitude of every moving shadow, but without disclosing their features, so that all these living beings looked like black cutouts against the horizon! Then the fire grew more intense; it divided and came from two directions at once toward the settlement. Papa ordered the women to leave, taking with them the children and old people. "The fewest things possible," he cried out to them. "Quick! . . . Leave your furniture . . . leave everything. . . ."

How astounded he now was at these women he had believed to be so docile! At first they did not want to leave the trenches they were digging alongside their men. Papa ran from one to the other, even grasping a few of them by the shoulders and shaking them a little.

Oh, those stubborn women! Once in their houses, they began collecting a hundred useless articles: mattresses, quilts, saucepans. "Is this the time to think of such things?" Papa angrily called out to them.

But they kept going back into their houses, one to collect her coffeepot, another a fine porcelain cup.

The farm wagons, the small two-wheeled carts, the buggies were piled high with domestic goods; upon these were perched the children, torn from their sleep, and now crying miserably, and hens that kept flying off, and young pigs. Women were hitching cows to the wagon tails. Never, so long as there remained a single movable object, would these insubordinate women have agreed to go. Papa ran about, whipping the horses at the head of the caravan. Terrified, they rushed toward the gap to the south, between the columns of fire which little by little were closing in on each other. Then Papa had the idea of setting fire to the crops to the north of the village. In this way fire would advance toward fire, and perhaps it would burn itself out. Such tactics had already succeeded on other occasions. He called Jan Sibulesky, one of the Little Ruthenians in whom he had always placed the greatest confidence, a man of judgment, quick to grasp what was sensible and make a rational choice.

"Quick," said my father to Jan Sibulesky, "take with you three or four men and, as soon as you can, set fire to the corners of all the wheat fields."

This was the moment when the Little Ruthenians gave every semblance of no longer understanding Papa. Jan as much as the others! Oh, the obstinate, greedy, silly men! In their own country they had possessed nothing — or so very little: a skimpy acre or two on the arid slopes of the Carpathians to feed an entire family; and they had left that behind them without too great pain. But now that they had all sorts of things — hay, sugar beets, wonderful wheat, full barns, really everything — they would not part with the least trifle.

"But if you want to keep everything, you'll lose everything," Papa told them.

And my father turned into something like a madman. He waved his arms, he shouted insults, thinking perhaps that the Little Ruthenians would at least understand those words. But the foolish wretches through all the thick smoke madly concentrated on pushing their plows around the settlement. Others carried water from the river to the houses to wet down the walls; still others drew pailfuls from the communal well, in the center of the village, which was deep and almost icy. Did they think that this water, so cold it clouded the outside of the pail, would serve better to cool the atmosphere than the water from the river? Then Papa tried to go by himself to set fire to the harvest, but the Little Ruthenians forcibly prevented him. Thus Papa realized that they had perfectly well understood his orders, that henceforth he was alone among his own people, as they were on their own against him. This loneliness in the face of danger made him despair. The heat was increasing. Occasional brands of fire flew over the village. A powerful roar filled the air. And everything was in fearful disorder; no longer was there anyone in charge, any obedience. Each man was wearing himself out in individual effort; a few simply awaited the fire, ax in hand. Then the flames at a single bound cleared one of the trenches; they took hold of a thatched roof; in an instant the house glowed with inner light. All was lost.

"Go, go!" Papa cried to the men. "You've only enough time to save yourselves!"

I have often envisioned Papa as he must have appeared that night, very tall with his arms stretched toward the sky, which outlined him also in black. What a terrible silhouette!

But now the Little Ruthenians were trying to save the burning house. So Papa moved toward them threateningly. He raised his hand, showed them the glowing heavens, and, in their own tongue, he asked them: "Don't you know what that means?"

All equally bewildered, they raised their heads toward the nightmare glow above them. Papa said that they looked like stupid birds turning their heads in unison toward an incomprehensible sign. And in their own tongue Papa told them what the sign meant: "The wrath of God! Do you understand? It is God's wrath!"

Then there took place something infinitely cruel. Understanding at last, all the men made ready to go — all except that Jan Sibulesky whom father had loved and often singled out as an example because of his never-failing judgment. Abruptly Jan rushed toward the chapel and emerged from it holding an icon of the Virgin. His icon in front of him like a shield, he walked toward the burning house. Papa at once understood what Jan was going to do. The flames illumined his face, his mouth, his forehead hardened in unshakable purpose, his blond beard, his blue eyes; in the full light big Jan marched forward, utterly visible; just as visible was the icon he carried, the icon of a Madonna with tender, childlike features. Thus brilliantly lighted, the eyes of the image shone as though they were alive.

"Stop, you idiot!" my father cried out to Jan.

But it was now a long while since anyone had obeyed him. His great mistake obviously, had been to speak of God's wrath. All his life my father believed that there had lain his crime: to have interpreted God, in a sense to have judged Him. Jan continued toward the flames, singing a hymn and holding the holy image just below his harsh face.

"You're going to die," Papa told him. "Stop him! Stop the poor fool!" he begged the others.

But they all stood like spectators, in a living hedgerow, and probably at that moment they were very curious about God and about Jan; so avid with curiosity that they were stripped of all other thoughts. The words of the canticle resounded for another moment above the crackling of the flames; then suddenly they changed into an appalling cry. Never could Papa erase from his memory, right upon the heels of the tones of prayer, this roar of horror. A blazing beam had tumbled upon Jan Sibulesky. The men who had been so intense upon miracles at last made up their minds to leave — and in a stampede. They sprang astride their horses, urging them on with sharp cries; they clambered onto the seats of the two-wheeled traps; they dashed out of the village, jostling each other. Papa begged them, as they passed him, to call out their names, for he could no longer recognize faces in the smoke, and he wanted to reassure himself that none of the Little Ruthenians would be left behind. "Get south," he yelled at each outfit as it passed by. In that direction, between the walls of fire, there was still a gap which, minute by minute, was visibly closing.

At last Papa jumped into his wagonette and, by the sound of the galloping horses, he tried to follow the caravan now hidden in the smoke. His vehicle, however, was too heavy to make enough speed over the stones and clods of earth. Papa at a bound put himself astride Dolly; then he got out his penknife and began to slash at the leather traces that attached the wagonette to the mare, reducing her speed. The traces were tough and hard to sever, but at last one came free, and then the other. Dolly went faster. The fire, though, was already raging here and there on the only route still open. Papa saw that Dolly by herself could get through quickly enough not to be burned, but that, burdened with a man, she certainly could not. From far up ahead one of the Ruthenians cried out to him to hurry. Papa called back that he needn't worry, he was coming. That was the last human voice he heard that night. Standing beside Dolly he gave her his orders: "Go . . . go . . . As for me, I still have the well of Dunrea; there — if I can get back to it — I'll be safe. . . . And I'm too tired, really too tired to go much farther. . . . The well will give me a bit of rest. . . ."

But that night no one was to obey him, not even his gentle, his obedient Dolly, for whom Papa, whenever he left Winnipeg on the way to his settlement, always took with him titbits and lump sugar.

So he raised his whip and struck Dolly a blow, on her most sensitive part, over the eyes. She went off neighing with pain and reproach. And, running, bending double to avoid the flames, Papa regained the center of Dunrea. His hair, his beard, his eyebrows were singed from the heat. He breathed as little as possible, holding a damp handkerchief over his mouth. He reached the edge of the well. Grasping the rope used to haul up the pails of water, Papa slid down into the deep, cool interior. He lowered himself to the level of the water. Almost at once the roar of the flames surrounded everything. All around the well the grass was afire. The rope likewise began to burn; Papa saw it come apart, strand by strand, in little spirals of ash. Quickly he pried out bricks, which were only loosely imbedded in the lining of the well; he dug himself a sort of niche, where he succeeded in finding a certain support. Then he cut the rope as high as he could. At just that moment he saw a shadow over the well opening, in perfect outline. He was greeted by a long-drawn-out neigh. "Oh Dolly!" cried my father, "Go . . . Go!" He ripped free a brick which he hurled at Dolly's head. Papa said that she leaned in to see whence came the furious voice and projectile. Then she reared and raised herself to a great height, head and mane erect. Papa began to smell the odor of burned flesh.

And he told how the inside of the well became broiling hot, the air so unbreathable that he had to go lower yet. He did it with the help of the rope, which he had tied to a stone projecting from the inner wall. He slipped into the water up to his knees, then to his waist. Half his body was freezing and numbed, while upon his head rained sparks of fire . . . and he thought that the end had really come. Papa said that he had been sure he was dead because suddenly nothing mattered to him any more. This was what gave him the deepest anguish when he thought back afterward: that everything, in the depth of the well, had become so dismal, so smothered, so extraordinarily silent. He had not thought of us; all he felt was quiet, so great a quiet that it was beyond resisting. These were his own words: "Neither regrets, nor hope, nor desires: a state of complete quiet." At the bottom of the well he barely could succeed in remembering life, having been alive. And how could he have the least taste for any return from so deep an indifference! Papa, believing himself dead, was a trifle astonished that death should be so gloomy, glacial, empty . . . and so reposing . . . that in death there should no longer be any affection possible. Within him there was a desert, just as above his head — in Dunrea — there was also a desert. . . .

The next morning the Little Ruthenians found him in the well.

When Papa opened his eyes on the desolation that was now the Lost River, he believed in Hell. Curiously, it was not with the furnace of the night before, with the outcries, with the unfollowed orders, that he was to associate Hell, but with this — a thick silence, almost inviolable, a dismal land, black everywhere, a dreadful death.

Raising himself up on the charred soil where they had laid him, Papa tried to give courage to his Little Ruthenians; since they had not lost their lives, they had not lost the essential thing. Neither he himself, however, nor the Little Ruthenians, had much further use for this essential thing. They said that they had, all the same, lost their lives, at least ten years of their lives. . . . And Papa remembered to ask about the women: "Are they all safe?" "Yes," the Little Ruthenians replied, "they are all safe, but weeping for their dear houses, their oaken chests, their chests full of fine linen. . . ."

Papa returned among us . . . and yet did he ever return? Appalled at his appearance, Maman asked him, "Has something happened to you, Edouard? What on earth has happened to you?"

But Papa merely put her off with an inconsequential account of what had taken place, how he had lost a settlement. For a long time that was all he ever admitted. Only to Agnès, when one evening she came and sat close beside him and looked at him tenderly — she was not afraid, never was afraid of his half-burned eyebrows — only to Agnès did he tell how he had once meddled with the business of explaining God to men; perhaps it was a day when he regretted not having remained in the depths of the well. . . . When Lazarus emerged from the grave, we have no knowledge that he was ever gay.

Still, there remained this most curious thing: Papa, become, as it were, a stranger to joy, so far removed from it that he was almost unable to recognize it in a human countenance, was nevertheless, sensitive to suffering.

Oh, here indeed was something that troubled us: when we laughed, when on occasion we succeeded in being happy, Papa was astounded! But let a misfortune, a sorrow strike one of us, then we saw Papa come alive . . . return to us . . . suffer all the more!

BAMBINGER
Mordecai Richler

We needed money. But we could not, like the Isenbergs next
door, put a "Room To Let" sign in the window. We had
standards to maintain.

"Taking in a refugee, a single man," my mother argued,
"would help to fight human suffering. It might also mean a
husband for Cousin Bessie, poor thing."

So in November, 1942, a phone call was made to the
proper agency, and we got our first roomer, a refugee, without
advertising. Herr Bambinger was a slight, stooping man with
a shiny bald head and almost no chin. He wore thick glasses
with steel frames and, even though he rolled his own
cigarettes, he used a tortoise-shell cigarette holder.

"I guess," my mother said, "you're thinking of settling
down. You'll be looking for a wife."

"You bet your bottom dollar he is," my father said.

On Friday Cousin Bessie was produced at dinner and on
Saturday my parents cornered Herr Bambinger.

"Beauty," my mother said, "is only skin deep."

"Ach, so."

"What a man wants in a wife is somebody steady," my
father said, offering Herr Bambinger a shot of apricot brandy.
"Somebody with a little something in the bank."

Herr Bambinger didn't, like the other refugees, drink black
coffee endlessly at the Old Vienna and pontificate about what
a dull, uncultured country Canada was. Bambinger spent most
of his evenings smoking in the dark in his room, the back
bedroom. He wrote a prodigious number of letters, always
filling the rice-paper pages from top to bottom with the
smallest, tightest handwriting I had ever seen. The letters
went to the International Red Cross and refugee organizations
and camps all over the world, but nothing ever came for him
unless it was his own letters returned or copies of the *Aufbau.*
Bambinger took a considerable interest in me. He convinced
my mother that comic books were a bad influence. Superman,
he said, was a glorification of fascism, and the Batman and
Robin had a thinly — "very thinly," he said — disguised
homosexual relationship. "I don't advise," he'd say to my

mother, "that the boy should go without a scarf in such coldness." A couple of days later it was, "The boy shouldn't keep the elbows on the table when he eats." Or, another time, as he switched off the radio abruptly, "A boy can't do his studies and listen to the wireless at the same time."

My parents believed that Herr Bambinger had my welfare at heart and when I protested against his intrusion they disciplined me. One Saturday afternoon my mother forced me to go out for a walk with Herr Bambinger.

"Why should I miss the ball game, but?" I asked.

"The poor man has a wife and child of your age and he doesn't know where they are or if they're still alive."

Bambinger — vengefully, I thought — led me to the art museum on Sherbrooke Street. "It is never too early," he said, lighting a cigarette, "for one to learn appreciation of the arts."

"How's about a cig for me?"

"Nicotine is bad for growing boys."

"If you're too cheap to butt me just say so."

"You are not only stupid. You are very impudent. If you were my boy it would not be so. I'd teach you respect."

"Well, I'm not your boy, see."

When Bambinger and I finally did tangle it was over coffee. Coffee, if you remember, was rationed during the war, and at the age of twelve a boy became entitled to a share. There were coupons for it provided in this book. I had waited impatiently for my twelfth birthday and the day after it I demanded a cup. My mother smiled a little. But Bambinger shot her a warning glance and regarded me reproachfully across the table.

"You know you're not allowed to drink coffee," my mother said. "You're still a child."

My sister grinned and took a long sip from her cup.

"As far as the legally elected government of Canada is concerned I am, as of yesterday, allowed to drink coffee."

"The government is full of anti-semites," my father pronounced compulsively.

But I could see that my mother's resolve was weakening.

"One cup," I pleaded. "Would it break your heart?"

"Your mother's right. Coffee is bad for a growing boy."

Staying up late, according to Bambinger, would also stunt my growth. As did evenings spent at the Park Bowling Academy.

"This is family business, so keep your big nose out of it."

"Apologize to Mr. Bambinger immediately."

"Either I get my legal ration or I destroy my coupons."

"You will do no such thing. Now apologize to Mr. Bambinger."

Bambinger smiled mockingly at me, waiting.

"Well, the hell with you," I shouted, turning on Bambinger. "Why'd you run away from Hitler, you chicken? Couldn't you have stayed behind and fought in the underground? Wouldn't that have been better than running out on your wife and kid to save your own skin?"

My mother slapped me.

"Okay," I said, bolting. "I'm leaving home."

Outside, it was raining. Fists jammed into my windbreaker pockets, hastily packed kitbag bouncing against my back, I jogged to the Park Bowling Academy, where Hershey was spotting pins. "Hey," I said, "how'd you like to run away from home with me?"

Hershey wiped the sweat from his forehead, pondering my proposition. "Cancha wait until Monday? We're having *latkas* for dinner tomorrow."

Walking back to St. Urbain with Hershey, I told him about my troubles with Bambinger. It began to rain harder and we sheltered under a winding outside staircase. "Hey, would you do me a favour?" I asked.

"No."

"*Thanks.*"

"What do you want me to do?"

I asked him to ring my doorbell and tell my mother I had fainted or something. "Say you found me lying in the gutter."

"You're chicken. I knew it. You're not running away from home."

Hershey gave me a shove and I scooped up my kitbag to slug him. He began to run. It was almost ten-thirty, the rain had turned to snow.

"You've come back," my mother said, seemingly overjoyed.

"Only for tonight."

"Come," she said, taking me by the hand. "We've just had the most wonderful news."

Bambinger was actually dancing round the dining-room table with my sister. He wore a paper hat and had let his glasses slip down to the tip of his nose. "Well," he said, "well, well, the prodigal returns. I told you not to worry."

Bambinger smiled and pinched my cheek, he pinched it very hard before I managed to break free.

"They were going to send out the police to look for you."

"Mrs. Bambinger and Julius are safe," my mother said, clapping her hands.

"They're coming here from Australia," my father said. "By ship. There was a telegram."

"I'm soaked. I'll be lucky if I didn't catch pneumonia."

"Yeah. Just look at him," my father said. "You'd think he'd been out swimming. And what did he prove? Nothing."

"I'll tell you what," Bambinger said, "you may still be too young for coffee but a little brandy won't hurt you."

Everybody laughed. Thrusting past Bambinger, I fled to the bedroom. My mother followed me inside. "Why are you crying?"

"I'm not crying — I'm soaked."

The dining-room vibrated with laughter.

"Go back to your party. Enjoy yourself."

"I want you to apologize to Mr. Bambinger."

I didn't say a word.

"You will be allowed one cup of coffee a week."

"Was that his idea?"

My mother looked at me, astonished.

"All right. I'm going. I'll apologize to him."

I went to Bambinger's room with him. "Well," he said

with an ironical smile, "speak up. I won't bite you."

"My mother says to tell you I'm sorry."

"Ach, so."

"You're always picking on me."

"Am I?"

"Maybe they don't understand. I do, but."

Bambinger rolled a cigarette, deliberately slow, and let me stand there for a while before he said, "Your grammar is atrocious."

"This is my room and my bed."

"Ach, so."

"It shoulda been anyway. I was promised. Only they made me stay with my sister and rented it to you instead."

"I think your parents need the money."

"I apologized. Can I go now?"

"You can go."

The next morning Bambinger and I couldn't look at each other and a week went by without his once admonishing, correcting, or trying to touch me. A thick letter came from Australia and Bambinger showed us photographs of a small, unsmiling boy in a foreign-type suit that was obviously too tight for him. His wife had stringy grey hair, a squint, and what appeared to be a gold tooth. Bambinger read passages from his letter aloud to my parents. His family, I learned, would not be arriving in Canada for six weeks, the boat trip alone taking a month.

Bambinger now applied himself entirely to work and frugality. He gave up smoking even hand-rolled cigarettes and put in overtime at the factory whenever it was available. On weekends Bambinger searched for bargains. One day he came home with a suit from a fire-sale for his boy and on another he purchased an ancient washing machine and set to repairing it himself. He picked up a table and chairs at an auction and bought a reconditioned vacuum cleaner at a bazaar. All these, and other articles, he stored in the shed; and all this time he ignored me.

One day I surprised Bambinger with a collection of

nearly new comic books — "For your kid," I said, fleeing — and the next morning I found them on top of the garbage pail in the shed. "Julius will not read such trash," he said.

"They cost me a nickel each, but."

"The thought was nice. But you wasted your money."

On Saturday afternoon, only a week before Mrs. Bambinger and Julius should have arrived, my father came into the kitchen carrying the newspaper. He whispered something to my mother.

"Yes, that's the name of the ship. Oh, my God."

Bambinger staggered in from the shed, supporting a table with three legs.

"Brace yourself," my father said.

Bambinger seized the newspaper and read the story at the bottom of page one.

"You can never tell," my mother said. "They could be in a lifeboat. That happens all the time, you know."

"Where's there's life, there's hope."

Bambinger went into his room and stayed there for three days and when he came out again it was only to tell us he was moving. The morning of his departure he summoned me to his room. "You can have your bed back again," he said.

I just stood there.

"You've been deprived of a lot. You've suffered a good deal. Haven't you? *Little bastard.*"

"I didn't sink the ship," I said, frightened.

Bambinger laughed. "Ach, so," he said.

"Why are you moving?"

"I'm going to Toronto."

That was a lie. Two weeks later I saw Bambinger walking toward me on St. Catherine Street. He was wearing a new suit, a fedora with a wide brim, and glasses with thick shell frames. The girl with him was taller than he was. At first I intended to ask him if he was ever going to come round for the stuff in the shed but I crossed to the other side of the street before he spotted me.

ALL THE SPIKES BUT THE LAST
F. R. Scott

Where are the coolies in your poem, Ned?
Where are the thousands from China who swung
   their picks with bare hands at forty below?

Between the first and the million other spikes
   they drove, and the dressed-up act of
   Donald Smith, who has sung their story?

Did they fare so well in the land they helped to
   unite? Did they get one of the 25,000,000 CPR acres?

Is all Canada has to say to them written in the Chinese
   Immigration Act?

Scott is addressing E.J. Pratt; the poem he refers to is "Towards the Last Spike", in which Pratt describes the building of the CPR.

ANGLOSAXON STREET

Earle Birney

Dawndrizzle ended   dampness steams from
blotching brick and   blank plasterwaste
Faded housepatterns   hoary and finicky
unfold stuttering   stick like a phonograph

Here is a ghetto   gotten for goyim
O with care denuded   of nigger and kike
No coonsmell rankles   reeks only cellarrot
attar of carexhaust   catcorpse and cookinggrease
Imperial hearts   heave in this haven
Cracks across windows   are welded with slogans
There'll Always Be An England   enhances geraniums
and V's for Victory   vanquish the housefly

Ho! with climbing sun   march the bleached beldames
festooned with shopping bags   farded flatarched
bigthewed Saxonwives   stepping over buttrivers
waddling back wienerladen   to suckle smallfry

Hoy! with sunslope   shrieking over hydrants
flood from learninghall   the lean fingerlings
Nordic nobblecheeked   not all clean of nose
leaping Commandowise   into leprous lanes

What! after whistleblow!   spewed from wheelboat
after daylong doughtiness   dire handplay
in sewertrench or sandpit   come Saxonthegns
Junebrown Jutekings   jawslack for meat

Sit after supper   on smeared doorsteps
not humbly swearing   hatedeeds on Huns
profiteers politicians   pacifists Jews

Then by twobit magic   to muse in movie
unlock picturehoard   or lope to alehall
soaking bleakly   in beer skittleless

Home again to hotbox   and humid husbandhood
in slumbertrough adding   sleepily to Anglekin
Alongside in lanenooks   carling and leman
caterwaul and clip   careless of Saxonry
with moonglow and haste   and a higher heartbeat

Slumbers now slumtrack   unstinks cooling
waiting brief for milkmaid   mornstar and worldrise

BACK DOOR, A One-Act Play
William Paluk

Key to Pronunciation

Anna Novak   *Ahn*-ah *Noh*-vahk
Halia (Helen)   *Hah*-lya
donyu (dearest daughter)   *doh*-nyu
Kritiuk   Krih-*tyook*
Znyva   Zhneh-*vah*
khroosty   *khroos*-teh

Cast

(In order of their appearance)

PETER KRITIUK   the baker
ANNA NOVAK   the mother
HALIA (HELEN)   the daughter
HENRY SMITH   the suitor
HENRIETTA SMITH   Henry's mother

SCENE 1

Scene: A kitchen, stage left, and a living-room, stage right, of a Ukrainian-Canadian home. Door out of living-room goes into bedroom. Door out of kitchen — that is, the back door — is the entry and exit of the play.

Peter: *(Knocks on door — shave-and-a-haircut, two bits.)* Baker!

Anna: Come in, Peter.

Peter: *(Enters, humming "Yes, My Darling Daughter".)* Hello, Mama Novak. Here's something for you on a beautiful spring day. *(Kisses her on nape of neck.)* Mmmm — ahhh.

Anna: *(Taken aback)* Hey! What kiss for? And from a baker! If I was young, I would slap.

Peter: That's to my future mother-in-law. One kiss on account.

Anna: Oh? On what kind account?

Peter: On account I'm in love with your daughter. And — know something? She's in love with me. Yeh, yeh. No foolin'.

Anna: *(Goes back to ironing. She's hard to excite.)* So? She in love. You in love. So I seen lots people in love. So leave extra rye bread today. Vladimir coming to dinner.

Peter: Is that all you can say? Look, Mama. All the world is upside down, and all you can say is "Vladimir coming to dinner". Ain't you got poetry in your soul?

Anna: I got lots work on my hands. *(Mildly curious)* You say Halia love you. How you know this?

Peter: Aha! You stopped ironing! Ha Ha! *(Mysteriously)* I know. I just know, that's all. Last night — oh, it was a beautiful night. Halia had a — a special kind of look in her eyes. I know, Mama. I know. *(Seriously)* Tell me something. What did she say to you this morning? Tell me, what?

Anna: I tell you. She get up as usual, and she say, "Hurry breakfast, Mama. No egg this morning. Just toast and coffee."

Peter: *(Sighs.)* That's Halia all right. Hiding her feelings. I can tell.

Anna: *(Back to her ironing)* Tell me one thing. You gonna leave me extra rye?

Peter: But she must have said or done something. Think, Mama Novak. Didn't you notice something — different — about her?

Anna: Ech . . . !

Peter: Think. Think!

Anna: Wait a minute. Maybe . . . but no, no . . .

Peter: *(Excited)* What was it? What was it? C'mon, c'mon. What?

Anna: Oh, just — she didn't eat her toast.

Peter: Aha! Didn't eat her toast. That's unusual, isn't it? Tell me the truth, Mama.

Anna: Mmmm . . . yeah. For Halia, unusual.

Peter: There! I told you. And you wouldn't believe me.

Anna: But, last night, did you ask her — anything?

Peter: We-e-ell, n-not exactly.

Anna: Did *she* say anything?

Peter: Er . . . n-no. Not really.

Anna: *(Sighs. Resumes ironing vigorously.)* Don't forget leave extra rye.

Peter: But you don't understand Halia like I do, Mama. I know how she feels, inside. I can tell by her face, her eyes. We ain't been goin' steady for a year and a half for nothin', Mama. But we got another date Saturday night. You wait. It'll all come out Saturday. Well, g'bye, Mama Novak.

Anna: G'bye, g'bye. Hey! You forgot extra rye bread.

Peter: *(Coming back)* Oh. You want an extra rye. Why didn't you say so, Mama? One extra rye comin' up. *(Leaves bread. Whistles "Wedding Invitatory Polka" as he departs.)*

SCENE 2

Scene: The same, a little later. Halia enters as her mother irons. It is obvious from her first words that she is indeed in love.

Halia: Hello, Mama.

Anna: Halia! Home already? Are you sick, *donyu*?

Halia: *(Leans against back door.)* You might call it that.

Anna: *(Relieved)* Mus' be. Standin' there, lookin' at ceiling. Take coat off and stay.

Halia: Oh. I forgot. Been forgetting things all day. That's why I'm home. I kept putting chocolate creams in the wrong boxes, so the boss told me to do him a favour and go home and get some sleep. But who wants to sleep?

Anna: What time you come home last night? Must be two — t'ree o'clock.

Halia: Oh, Peter and I got home early. Or-r, maybe it was late. In any case, I didn't get a wink of sleep last night.

Anna: *(Hums "Wedding Polka".)*

Halia: *(Recognizing it, focuses her look on her mother.)* What're you ironing, Mama? Hey! Those aren't our clothes. You're taking in Mrs. Macdonald's washing again. You clean her house — that should be enough.

Anna: *(Embarrassed)* You not supposed to see clothes.

Halia: But why do you do that? You don't have to take in anybody's washing! You have enough to live on, Mama.

Anna: You gonna need weddin' dress, maybe. And other clothes. I have pay for all my daughter weddings. I will pay for yours.

Halia: *(Runs to her, embraces her.)* Mama, you're the greatest! But — I haven't said anything about a wedding. How did you know?

Anna: I marry off eight children. I know.

Halia: *(Takes off coat. Drops it absent-mindedly on floor and sits dreamily on edge of kitchen chair.)* But you're right, Mama. Oh, it's so grand to be alive, and — and to be wanted. Such a heavenly feeling.

Anna: Everybody have heavenly feelin' today. Don't nobody feel . . . er . . . earthly?

Halia: Mama, you must have been in love once. I mean when you and Daddy met. What did it feel like? Tell me.

Anna: Well, let me see. Oh, I was young, and so pretty. Your father . . . well, we were immigrants. We had nothin'. We borrow money for licence. On weddin' night, your father got drun . . . got feelin' good, like you say. Then we have nine children in thirteen years. Yes — our marriage was earthly.

Halia: *(Laughs. Rises and hugs Anna.)* You know, Mama, I've read about boys asking girls to marry them. You see it on television. But when he asked me, sort of suddenly, well, I — I can't describe it.

Anna: *(Surprised)* He asked you? Already?

Halia: You could have knocked me over with a feather.

Anna: *(Shrugs shoulders.)* Ech! People in love!

Halia: When you love somebody very, very much — is that all you need? To get married, I mean.

Anna: Well, er . . . ech! How should I know? Go ask your sisters.

Halia: But I'm asking you! How would you size up a boy who wanted to marry me? Tell me. It's important to me what you think.

Anna: *(Pleased and flattered)* Oh. Important, huh? Well, he should have steady job. That important. And good heart. Good Ukrainian heart. Nice, but not too friendly. When he working, tell him no kissin' women. Kissin' not nice when he have wife at home.

Halia: I don't know what you mean. But I'm sure you'll like Henry.

Anna: I mean like today — I . . . like . . . *who?*

Halia: Henry. Henry Smith.

Anna: What . . . what dis . . . Henry Smit'?

Halia: Henry's the most wonderful man in the whole, whole world. We were having lunch yesterday. All of a sudden, right out of the blue, he asks me to marry him. Just like that! And he's serious, Mama. Dead serious.

Anna: *(Her temper is beginning to rise.)* Henry Smit', huh? And what's about Peter Kritiuk, the baker?

Halia: Peter? Oh, he'll be okay for some other girl. He's still a little immature, though.

Anna: O-o-oh? So you mature, huh? Well, come wit' me, mature daughter. *(Grasps Halia by the hand and pulls her to the living-room.)*

Halia: Mother! You're hurting my hand. Mama! You're hurting me.

Anna: I should hurt you in another place. Come here to bureau.

Halia: I'll come. Let go!

Anna: *(Drops Halia's hand when they face the old oak buffet.)* Now! Tell me, mature daughter, how many weddin' pictures on dis bureau?

Halia: I could have told you in the kitchen. There are eight. Eight wedding pictures.

Anna: *(Proudly)* Yes. Eight. Eight nice Ukrainian, some Polish, daughter-in-law and son-in-law. Today I have twenty-two grandchildren. In two months twenty-four.

Halia: Mama! Why all the statistics? I know them all.

Anna: Why? I tell why. Because you don't have brain in head. What's trouble wit' Peter?

Halia: Peter's not for me, that's all.

Anna: Henry Smit' not for you! What you t'ink, you English or somet'ing? Maybe you t'ink *I'm* English?

Halia: Henry's a Canadian, and so am I.

Anna: Aya! Can-a-dian! You see Canadian on — on boxcars, so you t'ink you Canadian. You . . . Ukrainian and he . . . English.

Halia: I . . . hadn't thought . . . about that part of it. *(Decisively)* Mama! You've got to do one thing for me. Promise. Please promise!

Anna: Forget dis Henry Smit' and I promise.

Halia: Mama! You've got to be fair. You haven't even met him. How can you say such a thing?

Anna: I can say. I mother.

Halia: And I love you very much. But you've got to meet him.

Anna: I don't got to not'ing.

Halia: Mother, I have a plan. Henry's coming to take me out tonight. You can meet him then.

Anna: How come he never be here before?

Halia: I told him I couldn't go out with him because I had a steady boyfriend. So we just had coffee breaks together and we had lunch every day for the last two weeks.

Anna: And from dis you want he should marry you?

Halia: It's hard to explain. It just happened. I can't explain it.

Anna: I can. You crazy. He crazy.

Halia: Mama, you must meet him and speak to him. I'll tell him to be here early. Then I'll pretend I'm getting ready upstairs, and you can talk to him and get to know him. Will you do that, Mama? Please promise.

Anna: (*Most unwillingly*) Yeh, yeh. Promise. I promise.

SCENE 3

Scene: The same, but there are crocheted antimacassars on sofa, ceremonial towels on pictures and buffet, the result of much preparation. It is evening. There is a knock on the front door.

Anna: Why he knock on front door?

Halia: (*From upstairs*) I forgot to tell him. You tell him, please?

Anna: (*Shouting through front door*) Go to back door!

Henry: (*Knocks on back door.*)

Anna: Come in, come in.

Henry: (*Enters, somewhat sheepishly.*) Good evening, Mrs. Novak. I'm . . . I'm Henry Smith.

Anna: (*Feigning surprise*) Oh. It's pleasure. We . . . we never use front door. (*Ushers him into living-room.*) You sit here on sofa and wait, please, for Halia to . . . er . . . finish dressing.

Halia: (*From upstairs*) Hi, down there. Is that you, Henry?

Henry: Right the first time.

Halia: I'll be a little while yet. Mind waiting?

Henry: Take your time, hon.

Anna: (*Sits on other 'end of sofa, and turns so she can face him*

squarely. Methodically she examines him, head to toe.) My! You are
. . . handsome boy. Thin, but handsome.

Henry: *(Still nervous)* Thank you . . . er . . . thank you, Mrs.
Novak, for that . . . that statement.

Anna: You have dark hair — almost like Ukrainian boy.

Henry: Er . . . all our family is dark.

Anna: *(Suddenly serious)* You have steady job?

Henry: No. I go to school — that is, university. But . . . I'll
be finished this year.

Anna: No steady job.

Henry: I . . . I'm majoring in business administration. But
my favourite subject is psychology.

Anna: You major . . . you . . . subject . . . but no job.

Henry: Nope. Maybe university *is* a kind of waste of time.
But Dad insisted.

Anna: *(Glad to get off unpleasant subject)* You Dad and Mother
— they both English?

Henry: Mom and Dad are both third-generation Canadians.
I've heard them say that.

Anna: Mmm hmmm. You know we all Ukrainian in this
house. *Many* generations Ukrainian.

Henry: Ukrainian. That's sort of Russian, or Polish, isn't it?
Or . . . what *is* Ukrainian?

Anna: *(Pleased for the first time)* Oh, you want to know where
is Ukraine. I show you. I bring from bedroom map. Excuse,
please. *(Vanishes into bedroom. Calls from there)* I have nice big
map here. *(Enters.)* Here is map of Ukraine. *(It is a big one,
and he has to move over.)* And here is Znyva, village where
husband and I born.

Henry: Sure is a big country. I suppose your country has lots of famous men. I've never . . .

Anna: *(Breaking in)* Famous men! You have heard of poet Shevchenko?

Henry: Shev-chen-ko. I do believe . . .

Anna: I show you. Wait! I go find something in trunk in bedroom. *(Vanishes, then returns with books.)* Here. One. Two. Three. Four. Four volumes poetry work by one man — famous poet Shevchenko. And you ask if we have famous men!

Henry: Well, while you were gone, I found the capital of your country. It's Kiev, isn't it?

Anna: Capital — Kiev. Now I get you book — beautiful colour book showing pictures of our capital. *(Vanishes again.)*

Henry: You haven't got the Encyclopaedia Britannica stashed away there somewhere, have you? Er . . . I'm just joking.

Anna: *(Enters, carrying volume.)* Here. Picture history of Kiev. Old capital. Beautiful. We have many songs about Kiev. Also about many other things. You have heard of Koshetz Choir?

Henry: I'm afraid to say it.

Anna: Some day, maybe, I will play you records. *(Henry is busily poring over map. Anna is pleased with the interest he has shown.)* But you *are* nice boy. I know many our boys who grow up in Canada not interested in our songs or history or poets. But *you* . . .

Henry: I'm not *really* interested in history.

Anna: No?

Henry: Well, that is, *this* is interesting. But I find Canadian history a little beyond me most of the time. It's so boring.

Anna: But you ask questions. That is interest. Yes, you *are*

70

interested. And I t'ink I like you. Only, if you are Ukrainian, it would be so nice.

Henry: Does Helen mind?

Anna: N-no. Halia not mind now. But later . . . You name Smit'. I know our boy name Pitkowsky, call himself Pitt. So you could be Smitkowsky. But no, no . . .

Henry: *(Picks up Kiev book. A letter falls out.)* Look! A letter just fell out of this book.

Anna: *(Takes the letter, unfolds it.)* It very old letter. My father — he dead now — he write me letter and I get it on my wedding day. Then I lose it. Now letter found again. *(She begins to sniff.)*

Henry: Sentimental value, eh, Mrs. Novak?

Anna: Oh, yes! Excuse me now, please. *(Hurries into kitchen, hand to eyes.)*

Halia: *(Enters.)* Well, here I am at last. Hope you weren't bored.

Henry: Hi, gorgeous. Your Mom and I had a nice long talk.

Halia: What's all this — books, map . . . ?

Henry: I asked your mother about her native country.

Halia: And you got your answer complete with map and illustrations.

Henry: Your mother said she likes me. *(They stand close together, looking into each other's eyes.)*

Anna: *(Enters, carrying bowl.)* Here some Ukrainian baking — khroosty. Sit down, sit down. Why you not sit down?

Halia: Mama, there isn't any room left on the chesterfield. *(Blackout)*

Scene: The same. It is the next day. Anna picks up telephone and dials.

Anna: Hello? Hello, Maria? This is you sister Anna. How rheumatism today? Oh, thank you, my side still bad, but at my age, what you expect — I don't go dancing no more . . . Well, this boy — this Henry Smit', come like I expect. We had talk. Nice boy, but not Ukrainian. No job. Dumb Dora, why she not fall in love wit' Peter Kritiuk? Oh. You think I should not try stop affair, eh? Don't make it out to be forbidden fruit, eh? Act like it okay, eh? But why? Oh. Halia may tire of boy. Yeah. That good idea. No, I not meet Mrs. Smit'. Hmmmm . . . drop in for coffee to Henry mother. Ech! I drink coffee when I have dinner. No time for coffee in between . . . what you mean I have old-country ideas? I see lots lady drop in to my Mrs. Macdonald for coffee. Maybe I will. Yes. Maybe tomorrow . . . I go shopping in morning, buy new hat, and drop in to Mrs. Smit' for coffee.

(Curtain)

SCENE 5

Scene: A telephone table and chair at stage right, in front of curtain. Henrietta Smith is on phone.

Henrietta: Hello, Agnes? This is Henrietta Smith. Sorry you couldn't make it for bridge last night. Your substitute was a Kay Wiggins from Grant Bay . . . I never could get onto her bidding . . . *(Back door gong sounds.)* Oh, hang on, Agnes. Someone's at the back door. Be right back — don't hang up, now. *(Walks across stage to door on stage left. Opens it, and Anna enters.)* Oh, hello.

Anna: Hello. You Meesus Smit'?

Henrietta: Yes, I am.

Anna: I Anna — Anna Novak.

Henrietta: Oh, you must be the new cleaning-woman. Thank heaven for that. It's a month since Katrina left, and the place is a mess. She told me she would try to find someone else.

Anna: You don't un'erstan'. My name Anna Novak, and my daughter . . .

Henrietta: Anna. That's enough. I never can get my tongue around your long surnames. Although I must say Novak is an easy one.

Anna: I drop in for coffee.

Henrietta: Of course you can have coffee. You go ahead and make yourself a cup. I'm on the phone, so I can't join you right now.

Anna: My daughter and you . . .

Henrietta: Take your time, and when you're ready you can start in the basement. Vacuum's in the hall closet. But it'll need tidying before you vacuum. *(Pause)* You understand me, don't you?

Anna: *(Defeated)* Yes. I un'erstan'.

Henrietta: Excuse me now, won't you, Anna? You go ahead and have your coffee now. The kitchen is right over there. *(Walks over to stage right and picks up phone.)* Hello, Agnes? That was the new cleaning-woman. Name of Anna Novak. Clean-looking. *(In undertone)* But you should see the hat! Looks like a wet towel with purple plums all over it. Now, this hand I held last night . . . *(Anna exits.)* I held nine spades, and as it turned out, Kay had three. So my opener was three spades. But how could we know the ace was out against us?

73

(Looks out through window.) Agnes, I can't understand it. The new cleaning-woman has just left. Told me she wanted coffee, then ups and leaves. Ah, I know. She took one look at my basement and quit. And I can't really blame her. But about this hand I was holding . . .

(Blackout)

SCENE 6

Scene: Same as Scene 3. It is evening of the same day. Anna is stacking clothes in a wicker basket. Halia enters.

Halia: Hi, Mama.

Anna: Hello, *donyu.*

Halia: *(Takes off coat, hangs it in closet, and sees hat box. Mystified, she takes the hat out of the box.)* A new hat, Mama! *(Anna reacts. She had forgotten to hide it.)* What is the occasion?

Anna: *(Confused)* Oh . . . I just buy it. But I do not like. Will take back.

Halia: *(Fits hat onto Anna's head.)* You bought it for some reason, Mama. Tell me.

Anna: *(Sits down and removes hat. She is now resigned to telling truth.)* I bought it to go have coffee with Henry mother.

Halia: With Mrs. Smith? You didn't say anything.

Anna: It was to be surprise to you.

Halia: And what happened?

Anna: She thought I was new cleaning-woman. Said I should clean house.

Halia: I don't believe it. How did it happen? Tell me.

Anna: I went to the back door and rang bell and she came to door and said . . .

Halia: Back door? Why the back door, Mama?

Anna: What is matter with back door? I always go in back door.

Halia: *(Leans against chair for support.)* Yes. Yes, of course. You — always go in the back door. *(She goes to Anna, puts her arms around her, kisses her.)* And I love you, Mama. I love you very, very much, and I'll never leave you, never!

Anna: You· will. You will. You want marry dis Henry Smit', no?

Halia: *(In tears now)* Henry? O — I barely knew him. It was just one of those things. A girl is allowed to have *some* silly ideas, isn't she?

Anna: I pay seven dollars and half for new hat.

Halia: It's a gorgeous hat. It makes you look smart and young. Wait . . . *(With decision)* just wait till Peter Kritiuk sees it!

(Curtain)

SCENE 7

Scene: As in Scene 5. Henrietta is on phone.

Henrietta: Hello, Helen Novak? This is Henrietta Smith. May I speak with your mother? Oh, she's not feeling well. Henry told me about what happened this morning. I'm phoning to apologize for being so stupid. Will you tell her that I am truly, deeply sorry? Your mother came to the back door and I . . . never for a moment . . . thought of her being your mother. Would you tell her that Mr. Smith and I would be pleased and honoured to drop in and see you both at your home some time soon? Do please tell her.

(*Blackout*)

SCENE 8

Scene: Curtain rises on same set as Scene 6. Later that evening. There is a knock on the door. Halia opens it and Henry enters. Halia turns face away as Henry tries to kiss her.

Henry: I don't get it, hon.

Halia: I tried to make it clear on the phone, Henry. Let's face it. It's all over with us. It's not as bad as all that — people break up every day.

Henry: I won't listen to any more of this. What you're saying is nonsense. What about the things we talked about — a home, a family?

Halia: They were just dreams. Some dreams don't come true.

Henry: You've been reading the wrong paperbacks. Look. We love each other. We're free, white, and twenty-one. So what's the natural thing to do?

Halia: For my mother — to enter a house by way of the back door.

Henry: But I don't want to marry your mother!

Halia: She comes in the same package. You order one, you get the other free.

Henry: So you get a mother from my side. So we're even. Now, let's start where we left off . . .

Halia: Uh-uh. It's got to be a clean break. No sentimental slush.

76

Henry: *(Unbelievingly)* You're serious!

Halia: Marriage is serious.

Henry: Look, honey. What's most important? It would have been nice if our mothers had been compatible. Okay. So they're not. So let's look at us.

Halia: You lost me away back. I'm still looking at our mothers. Mine is very important to me.

Henry: What about me? Remember me?

Halia: Oh yes, I do.

Henry: Then what's the problem?

Halia: Mama's happiness matters to me. You can't build your own happiness on someone else's misery. Especially if that someone else is your mother.

Henry: I'll make you forget your worries, everything. Give me a chance.

Halia: How long would that last? Till our honeymoon was over. Then we'd have to come back and face facts. I couldn't stand my mother's rejecting me . . . or you . . . *(Cries.)*

Henry: I'm sorry you have to cry. I haven't seen you cry before.

Halia: It's nothing. I'm especially good when I peel onions.

Henry: *(Doesn't know which way to turn. He reaches for his hat and turns to the door, then turns back and holds out his hand uncertainly.)* Then it's goodbye. *(She comes to him and takes his hand, but the next moment they are crushed in each other's arms. She pulls herself free and turns away. Henry's voice seems suddenly mature.)* One thing. This clean break business — that's your idea. I still think we could work it out. And if you change your mind about our date tonight, I'll be waiting at the drugstore. *(Exits.)*

Anna: *(Appears in bedroom doorway. Halia rushes into her arms, sobbing.)* I know, I know . . .

Halia: I'll get over it, Mama.

Anna: Come over to sofa, *donyu*. I want speak with you.

Halia: I don't want to talk about — him.

Anna: Not about him, *donyu*. About my own father. You know he dead a long time. But many year ago, when I young girl like you back in Carpathian Ukraine, he love me like I love you today. He want me to stay wit' him in old country, but I want go away, see new world. We had quarrel. But I stubborn. I sail away to Canada. He never write.

Halia: Never?

Anna: Not for very long time. Then one day I write I am getting married in Canada. On my wedding day, I get dis letter from my father. Henry found letter in Kiev book. It lost t'irty year.

Halia: Thirty years!

Anna: I will read you little bit. *(Reads)* "At home in mountains are bighorn sheep. Young mountain sheep go fast to very top of mountain, see green pasture far away, and leave flock for new grazing ground. But old sheep cannot climb high. Must stay in lower pasture, and graze there. So I am old. I cannot go high up any more. But you, Anna, you young. You climb higher and higher till you young feet carry you to top of mountain. And only you can see new distant pasture land, green and beautiful. So," my father write, "go, Anna, climb high as you can. I old and must stay below. I can no more help you, my child, but I can wish you Godspeed."

Halia: He *did* forgive you, Mama — and on your wedding day.

Anna: Yes, but when letter found, it come like a message from God to me.

Halia: Message?

Anna: Yes. For you, Halia. Now it is I who am too old to see new future. But you are young, and future belong to young.

Halia: Mama, I won't listen any more.

Anna: Yes, you will listen. And you will go to you Henry Smit'.

Halia: But . . .

Anna: And not tomorrow or next week — tonight.

Halia: I don't know what to say . . .

Anna: You say not'ing. Just go.

Halia: (*Looks searchingly at her mother, then speaks with decision and joy.*) I will, Mama. I'll go to him.

Anna: And Godspeed, my child.

(*Curtain*)

Wedding Invitatory Polka

IN THE WILDERNESS
Al Purdy

On the road to Agassiz in winter
of 1962
grandfathers
         young wives
               old children
marching in the savage demolitions of hunger
for their own people
to the mountain prison at Agassiz
where incendiarist husbands and
incandescent nephews and
sons of that pale yellow soap-like stuff
         which is dynamite
are locked away near a town named
for the gentle naturalist
         Louis Agassiz
In a way unrealized
these are the Children of Israel
with a Pillar of Fire by day
and a Pillar of Fire by night
standing over them in the mountains
In this wilderness
of 1962
we are all around them
(Big Fanny with sore feet slapping
onto the gravel road
Pete Elasoff with rock bruises
the old men with prophets'
beards and a Pillar of Fire
by day standing over them
on the Hope-Princeton highway
and stirrings of gravel sliding
down in the deep blue misted morning
are the trickling afterbirth of mountains) —
Note for historians:
we have set up by-laws for snares and
        deadfall regulations to trap them

the roads are shadowy with swaying nooses
          of municipal officials
the highways are luminous with Mounties and
road blocks and vote-catching grins of
          ambitious attorney generals
riding all night against these shivering foot soldiers
          slogging at dawn thru the frosty ranges —

Sitting at Agassiz with Big Fanny
in 1963
talking with Big Fanny at Agassiz
while the Mounties' "D" squad
drives by in Chevys and Pontiacs
continually hovering
talking of young Podmoroff who died
in Agassiz mountain prison and
was buried home in the Kootenays
talking of 100 men fasting and dying
in Agassiz mountain prison
the sons of mothers and daughters of husbands
and Big Fanny:
"I was 15 days on water and lemon and
now apple and prune juice"
(40 days and 40 nights in the wilderness
while the "D" squad looked and hovered
and the Pillar of Fire by day
stood over the Sons of Freedom at Agassiz)
Talking with Big Fanny
about the mystic Lebedoff
comic-opera-satan-Lebedoff
Judas-enemy of Peter Verigin's people
who plots against them in the far mountains
schemes at Wynndel
          for the people's destruction
accepting another 30 pieces of silver smiling and
the Mounties' "D" squad cruising and hovering —

(Talking to Big Fanny
making notes for an article
I think of coeval saints and ascetics and
the ordinary people with such
bright illusions of extraordinary freedom those
troublemakers of God:
could you find one in a nightclub for instance walking
across the floor and changing
                            — changing?
And how can they ever be sure they are
            what they seem to become?
Stand up straight where the lights are glaring
bright with microphones and flashbulbs and everyone
screaming and listening and people saving
your bathwater to sell for two bucks a bottle and
raffling off your dirty underwear
at the next scheduled crucifixion and
the eyes of gentle people turning animal
— I wonder how it feels to have your plodding
pedestrian mind sprout wings and fly
handsome as an actor playing Icarus
toward the cold sun truth) —

Talking with Big Fanny
at Agassiz in 1963 sitting
on an old blue mattress cover
and she with her shoes off talking
and talking of Judas-Lebedoff
plotting against them at Wynndel
talking of exile on Piers Island
in the Gulf of Georgia in 1932
and Fanny in Kingston Pen
for 3 years in 1947-50
(did they allow her to go barefoot?)
sitting on an old blue mattress cover

with Florence Storgoff in 1963
and a Pillar of Fire by day
shining over the mountains at Agassiz
while shanties of old Kotex boxes
covered with waterproof plastic
are built near the dusty road
and the children flash by in
the running games of children laughing
and the old men with prophets' beards
stand in the road with pamphlets —
And I write in a steno's notebook
as the tourists watch and wonder
and I drink some applejuice thinking
watching the busty young females
that my thoughts are not ascetic and
Florence Storgoff all 250
pounds of her talks of persecution
and religious freedom on a side road
near Agassiz in 1963 —
And the old men sing in a strange tongue
in sorrow's language over the darkening
landscape of fir trees and mountains and tremulous
whispering voices of the night animals
boom in the swamp and night birds cry over
snick of rifle bolts —
And down the road the prisoners are dying
the young hunger strikers are dying little by little —
But I am not one of them
I am not one of these people
nor do I wish to be —

But remember their names
Verigin Elasoff Podmoroff and Big Fanny
        (with sore feet hurting)
the jubilant bombers and blazing incendiarists

the nay-sayers and Spirit Wrestlers of the Kootenay
with the Mounties' "D" squad cruising and hovering
and overhead where the mist surrounds them
a Pillar of Fire or a flash of lightning
a Pillar of Fire or only the prison floodlights —

Verigin Elasoff Podmoroff and Big Fanny
and we stand around in the wilderness watching
and we are the wilderness
                    Remember their names —

A WEDDING IN TORONTO

Austin C. Clarke

"A police coming in a man's house, and at a wedding
reception, to boot! and breaking up a party? Merely because
some old can't-sleep bitch next door, or down-below can't find
a man, or something? What kind o' place, what sort o' country is
this? It never happened in Barbados, and it never could.
Imagine a police in Barbados, coming into a man's house,
during a party, and a wedding party at that, to tell that man
he is making too much noise! Man, that policeman's arse
would be so stiff with lashes, he would never do that again! A
police coming into a man's apartment, and breaking up a
wedding reception because some old bitch who can't sleep,
complained?" Boysie never got over the shock of seeing the
policeman at the door, standing like a monument to
something, with an untranslatable expression on his face, with
one hand resting perhaps absent-mindedly on the holster of his
gun, and the other, raised and caught in the slow-motion
paralysis of knocking on the apartment again. It was a loud,
firm knock of authority. The wedding guests were, at that
time, in the middle of the speeches; and Boysie, who was the
master of ceremonies, had been saying some amusing things
about marriage. It was at the point when he was saying, *Ecce
homo*, over and over again, (using his best stentorian, oratorical
Barbadian dialect), exhorting them, as: "La-dies and
gentlemen! ladies and gentlemen too! greetings and
salutations, because on this most auspicious of evenings, on
the aurora of long and felicitous matrimony, I say to you, to
you, ladies and gentlemen, I say, *ecce homo,* behold the man!
ecce homo, here I stand!" (Freeness, dressed to kill, in a
three-piece suit; Matthew Woods, spic and span; Estelle,
beautiful as a virgin, as a star; and many others, crammed into
the happy apartment, screamed for joy, when Boysie began
this speech, his fifth for the afternoon's festivities. Each
wedding guest including Agatha, the bride and Henry, the
bridegroom, had made a speech. Some had made two speeches.
Boysie had made his first, about an hour after the wedding
party returned to the apartment. It was five o'clock then.

Now, after many toasts and speeches and eats and drinks, Boysie was captivating his audience again. The time was midnight. The guests liked it; and they bawled and told Boysie they liked it. Henry, sober and married; Agatha, turning red, and flushed, and happy, and drunk as Dots, Boysie's wife, was, held her head back and exposed her cavities filled with silver, and said, "I could have another wedding reception like this, tomorrow! One like this every month!") "I say to you, ladies and gentlemen, I say, *ecce homo,* behold the man! *ecce homo,* here I stand! Here I stand, ladies and gentlemen, with a glass of drink in my hand, wherewithal for to mitigate the aridity of my thirst. And as I have arisen from my esteemed seat this fifth time, and as I have quoth to you, *bon swarr,* or goodevening, to the ladies and to the gentlemen of this nocturnal congregation of celebrating wedding guests, I say it again, for its sincerity can bear much repetition, *bon swarr,* my dear Agaffa, goodevening, Henry, you lucky old Bajan bastard!" And it was here, in the roar of acceptance by each person in the room, when they held their glasses up, and Boysie's glass was held right there, at the correct angle, that the knock brutalized the apartment. Its suddenness made them notice it. But they had no suspicions. Boysie said, with his glass still raised, "Perhaps, ladies and gentlemen, it is some poor suppliant wanting warmth of this nocturnal congregation." And he moved away, towards the door, his drink still in his shaking hands, to invite the person inside to partake of the hospitality. Bernice went to Agatha to fix the veil on her dress, and therefore, fortunately, blocked her vision of the police officer at the door, with his hand on his holster. Boysie didn't lose his aplomb. The police officer was very polite to him. "Break it up, soon, buddy. It's past midnight, and the neighbours're complaining about the noise."

Boysie was going to offer the officer a drink, but he changed his mind.

"Don't let me get another report that you making noise, eh? Break it up, soon, buddy."

Boysie did not move from the door until the officer of the

law walked back to the elevator; and he did not move until he saw him get into it; and Dots, who by this time had put a record on the machine the moment she heard the officer's voice, was now standing beside Boysie, like a real wife, supportingly.

"And the poor girl's enjoying herself so much! And on her wedding day? Jesus Christ, these people is savages; man, they're damn uncivilized! You mean to tell me, on the girl's wedding day?" Boysie put his arm round Dots's new, shiny, almost bare shoulder, and he squeezed her a little bit, and said, "We going party till that bitch come back!" Boysie left her, and went to Bernice and whispered in her ear, "The police!" Bernice grew tense. "But only me, and now you, and Dots know. So keep it dark. Keep it dark. We got to go on. How the hell could we ask the people to leave? How would Agaffa feel? How would Henry feel, on his wedding night, to boot?"

But Boysie and Dots and Bernice made certain not to make Agatha and Henry feel the tension that had begun to creep into the party. It was impossible to recapture the gaiety and the enjoyment that was present before the policeman knocked on the door. Dots would have had the guests leave immediately; after a respectable drink; she would have insisted upon it, because Agatha and Henry had to go on their honeymoon, to Niagara Falls. But Boysie said no. "This is a wedding. Not any old damn party with beatniks." And he left Dots standing there, arguing the wisdom of his suggestion with Bernice; and he went to the record player; (this record player had arrived from Eaton's department store two hours before the wedding reception began; delivered on a hire-purchase, the monthly payments of which were fifty-five dollars and twenty-five cents; and which Dots did not know how she would meet; but the sound was high and high-fidelity and stereophonic too, and the beauty and the loudness of the sound allayed their fears of having the machine repossessed. "Man, let we play the thing for today, then; and enjoy it, and then see what happen, man!" And Boysie agreed to that;

although before Dots said so, he had already agreed, in his mind, to keep the record player). Boysie now selected a calypso by the Mighty Sparrow, *Shanty Town People*: in which Sparrow was complaining of having to move out of his comfortable apartment, in Trinidad, because people from the slums had encroached on his location on the hill. The music raged, as the spirits in the guests and in the drinks raged. Estelle was beautiful in her wedding-party dress. She was thinking of the closeness she herself had come to marriage. And more than once, during the hectic afternoon and night, she wondered where the hell her man, Sam Burrmann, was, at this happy time. But by now, she had put him out of her mind, and she devoted all her body and energy to Matthew Woods, who shook his body in dance, as if he was in some mad trance. *Sunday morning, they fighting, they drinking, they beating pan . . . send for the police, still the bacchanal won't cease.* It was a royal time: it was an ironic time, to have a calypso reproduce the exact conditions of a party at which the police had come. And judging by the hour hand, it was Sunday morning too! But no one cared for Toronto, or police, or the neighbours: this was a wedding; and as Dots said, "A person can only get married one time. Even if he divorce and marry a second time, the second time don't seem to be like the first time! So the first time *is* the time!" Boysie was dancing with her. Brigitte had held on to Freeness the whole day, probably by design; probably by the suggestion of Boysie (whose woman she was); Boysie, who, now in the castle of skin and pride, in his briar patch of host and wedding-giver, had no time for outside-women; and Bernice was dancing with a man who nobody knew, who nobody invited, but who was treated with the same courtesy and hospitality as the bridegroom, as if he was the bride's father. Agatha's father hadn't arrived yet. Agatha's mother hadn't arrived yet. Agatha's friends, Agatha's many friends from the university, and her lawyer-friend (all of whom had been sent invitations — that was Boysie's personal gift to the couple) hadn't arrived yet. It was a sorrowful sight, at the church, when it was found out that no one was sitting on the bride's side of witness and evidence. Dots quickly saw the situation developing, and quickly saw the embarrassment it would cause to Agatha when she arrived sweet and young, virginal and white, in her long dress, to glance over the wide expanse of the desert of her friends. And Dots ushered and re-ushered half of the church over to Agatha's side. When the organ roared and snorted through the Wedding March, everybody was laughing, even Agatha. Reverend Markham was happy. The choir was in good voice, loud when it was supposed to be loud, soft when the organist breathed with the organ, and whispered that the choir be like a piano, pianissimo. But when they were in the office, signing away their lives and their promises to one another, Dots stood like a mother-hen on the top steps of the church, directing the people (those who didn't have cars) to cars, and warning the photographer who had arrived late, "Look here! don't take the whole day, hear? We have things waiting at the wedding reception." And after that, she whispered in Bernice's ears, "It's a shame, a great burning shame that that bastard, Agatha's father, thinks he is too great and too proud to come and witness his own daughter on her wedding day. A person does only have one wedding day in her life, and that bastard didn't even come. He didn't come."

"And the mother ain't turned up yet, neither."

"Bernice, gal, you are seeing the ways o' white people this lovely autumn day. The ways o' white people. They would kill their own flesh-and-blood just to prove a point."

"It is sad, though."

Estelle had overheard, and she said, "They love one another, though, Agatha and Henry. And they won't be living at the parents."

"Still a blasted shame!"

And now, at the reception, nobody apparently tired, after so many hours of eating and drinking and dancing, with the problems of *Shanty Town People* being reproduced for them, by the visit of the policeman, and by the record itself, these West Indians and one white woman, ("She's a Wessindian now, gal!

We claim her now that her people and her parents let her down. Gorblummuh, we is one people who don't reject nobody through prejudice."): . . . *I tired and I disgust . . . big Sunday evening, they cussing, they fighting, they gambling, they beating pan and bup-bup!-iron bolt, and stone pelting, send for the police, still the bacchanal won't cease.* . . . There were fifty people invited to the reception. They were fifty people in the two-bedroom apartment from five o'clock. They are fifty-one people (with the uninvited man), in the apartment now, at one-thirty, Sunday morning. Boysie has his arms in the air, and is dancing as if his body has been seized by some voodoo, or St. Vitus dance mood; Dots has thrown one brocaded expensive slipper somewhere in a corner, and she is jumping up. The record, a favourite with everybody in the room, is put on again. It is put on three times, four times, five times, six times; and Boysie says, on the seventh time, "Man, play that thing a next time, do!" And it is put on the eighth time. . . . *and big Sunday morning, they cussing they fighting they gambling; they beating pan and bup-bup!-iron bolt and stone pelting, send for the police, still the bacchanal won't cease, so they violent so they fast, they better go back to their mansion on the Labasse.* . . . A smudge of fatigue and sweat walked imperceptibly from under Estelle's hairy armpits. Bernice noticed it; and she took Estelle into Dots's bedroom, and rubbed some of Dots's under-arm deodorant, "Ban", on the story-telling odour. Estelle smiles, and dashes back out to dance. Agatha, with the first signs of marriedhood and possessiveness, sits and watches Henry dance with Pricilla, the nurse ("But who the hell invited Pricilla in here, in my decent place, eh? Boysie you invited Pricilla?"); and Agatha watches him, and she watches Pricilla's sterilized nurse's hips, as they do things with the rhythm that she herself, legal and wedded to Henry for better and for worse, cannot do. Some men are in the kitchen, eating, as they have been doing since five o'clock in the afternoon. There is a big argument going on, about cricket. None of these men has seen a cricket match, in five years, not since they left their islands.

But they are arguing about Sir Frank Worrell, and the cover drive he made off Alec Bedser at Lords in 1950, many many years ago. One man says, "The English think they great? They playing they're great? But be-Jesus Chroist, when Worrell, when Sir Frank leaned into that out-swinging from Bedser hand, gorblummuh, like lightning it went to the bound'ry for four. Right offa Worrell's wrist; and you-all know, Worrell, Sir Frank, is one man with more wrist than, than, — than Boysie in there, have stones in his underwears!" And like a contagion, everybody bawled, and poured himself another, larger rum. The record is changed. Sparrow is talking about his boyhood. The men dropped their glasses and ran for the women. They reached out their hands, and lifted the dripping, shining, shiningly-dressed, rouged-and-perfumed-smelling tired women off their chairs. Boysie is dancing with Dots, as if they are lovers: close. His brilliantined head, which had sweated for hours, for hours, under his stocking-top, is sleeked down and shining; and Dots's hairdo, done amidst pain and time, talk and gossip in Azan's beauty parlour, the previous Thursday, when the shop was noisy and filled with domestics and talk about "this rich-rich Jewish girl who is marrieding with some Bajan bastard, by the name of Henry-something, Christ I wonder if she really have rocks inside her head! She couldn' find nobody better?" Dots had listened, and had held her peace: they did not really know the facts. *Now, I am a rebel, I seeking my revenge any kind o' way, I'm a devil. I don't laugh, I don't smile, I don't play. . . .* Boysie is not smiling. He is holding Dots so close but she is his wife and he, her husband. . . . *Anytime we meet, man-to-man, it's blood and sand!* Estelle thinks of the time when Bernice and Dots and Boysie had come to the room on Bedford Road, and had found her delirious with fever and misery and thoughts that could not be achieved; and how they dressed her; how they paid the landlord the rent owing, which Matthew Woods had sworn he wanted to pay for her, but which she told him not to pay, because she didn't want to be obligated to another man; and how they had driven her back to Boysie's and Dots's apartment and here, she had slept, the first good night's rest in such a long time. She is thinking of Bernice, her dear sister, and of her bad luck: "that woman, Mrs. Burrmann thinks she can solve anything by treating my sister so rotten? But let her wait till I get more strength, till I have this baby, well, be-Christ, if I don't go right up there in Forest Hill for her arse! Her husband, Sam Burrmann could breed me, and then she could fire my sister from her job!" And Estelle thinks too of the future: hers and Bernice's. "What is my sister going to do? I left Barbados, and come all the way up here, and spoil things for that girl!" And she thinks of the present. There is a man standing before her. He is the man who nobody invited. He is standing in front of her like a threat, like a challenge. He wants to dance with "the prettiest lady in this place". The compliment is sincere, and Estelle stands up, just as Sparrow says, *They treat me like a savage, of me they took advantage; when I was young and growing up in town, all o' them bad-johns used to knock me down.* . . . A tear is crawling like perspiration down Estelle's face. The man does not notice. He has his mind on other parts of her anatomy.

It was then, that the second knocking was heard, on the apartment door. Boysie went to the door. The same policeman, plus another, were standing there. "I told ya," the first policeman said. There was no anger in his voice. He seemed peeved that someone would report noise twice in one night; he seemed as if he had been awakened from his slumbers in some dark alley in the dark city; as if he had been roused from a poker game somewhere down in the jungle of apartments near by. Boysie knew what to do. The guests began leaving right away. Everybody except those who were staying for the night, those who lived there: Boysie and Dots and Bernice and Estelle. Henry looked at the policemen and said things in his heart, which if they were audible would have given him a beating and then a long jail term. Agatha was crying. She was still in her wedding gown; Henry in his formal morning suit. The policemen waited until every one of the guests left. As Agatha, walking beside Henry, along the long corridor, as if she was still walking that interminable aisle up the aisle to face the altar and the cross and the Maker and Reverend Markham, women with curlers in their hair, peeped through open doors; and just as the policemen entered and went down into the half-awake apartment building, in the elevator going out, one white woman, in a torn pink nightgown, which showed the blackness between her thighs, sneered, "You white bitch! You white trash!" and slammed her apartment door. The others, among the onlooking guard of honour and dishonour, shook their heads, and did not slam their doors: but nobody knew what they were saying in their hearts, behind their closed doors. In all the confusion, in all the disappointment and crying (Dots and Bernice and Estelle remained sitting on the large, new couch, crying for Agatha's sake; and Agatha herself, in tears, had just wet their cheeks with the tears of her kisses), the record player was still commenting: *They treat me like a savage . . . they treat me like a savage . . . they treat me like a savage . . . they treat me like a savage . . . they treat me like a savage. . . .* The needle was stuck in a groove of the record.

A CLASS OF NEW CANADIANS
Clark Blaise

Norman Dyer hurried down Sherbrooke Street, collar turned
against the snow. "Superb!" he muttered, passing a basement
gallery next to a French bookstore. Bleached and tanned
women in furs dashed from hotel lobbies into waiting cabs.
Even the neon clutter of the side streets and the honks of
slithering taxis seemed remote tonight through the peaceful
snow. *Superb,* he thought again, waiting for a light and
backing from a slushy curb: a word reserved for wines, cigars,
and delicate sauces; he was feeling superb this evening. After
eighteen months in Montreal, he still found himself freshly
impressed by everything he saw. He was proud of himself for
having steered his life north, even for jobs that were menial by
standards he could have demanded. Great just being here no
matter what they paid, looking at these buildings, these faces,
and hearing all the languages. He was learning to be insulted
by simple bad taste, wherever he encountered it.

Since leaving graduate school and coming to Montreal, he
had sampled every ethnic restaurant downtown and in the old
city, plus a few Levantine places out in Outremont. He had
worked on conversational French and mastered much of the
local dialect, done reviews for local papers, translated
French-Canadian poets for Toronto quarterlies, and tweaked
his colleagues for not sympathizing enough with Quebec
separatism. He attended French performances of plays he had
ignored in English, and kept a small but elegant apartment
near a colony of *émigré* Russians just off Park Avenue. Since
coming to Montreal he'd witnessed a hold-up, watched a
murder, and seen several riots. When stopped on the street for
directions, he would answer in French or accented English. To
live this well and travel each long academic summer, he held
two jobs. He had no intention of returning to the States. In
fact, he had begun to think of himself as a semi-permanent,
semi-political exile.

Now, stopped again a few blocks farther, he studied the
window of Holt Renfrew's exclusive men's shop. Incredible, he
thought, the authority of simple good taste. Double-breasted

chalk-striped suits he would never dare to buy. Knitted sweaters, and fifty-dollar shoes. One tanned mannequin was decked out in a brash checkered sportscoat with a burgundy vest and dashing ascot. Not a price tag under three hundred dollars. Unlike food, drink, cinema, and literature, clothing had never really involved him. Someday, he now realized, it would. Dyer's clothes, thus far, had all been bought in a chain department store. He was a walking violation of American law, clad shoes to scarf in Egyptian cottons, Polish leathers, and woolens from the People's Republic of China.

He had no time for dinner tonight; this was Wednesday, a day of lectures at one university, and then an evening course in English as a Foreign Language at McGill, beginning at six. He would eat afterwards.

Besides the money, he had kept this second job because it flattered him. He was a god two evenings a week, sometimes suffering and fatigued, but nevertheless an omniscient, benevolent god. His students were silent, ignorant, and dedicated to learning English. No discussions, no demonstrations, no dialogue.

I love them, he thought. They need me.

He entered the room, pocketed his cap and earmuffs, and dropped his briefcase on the podium. Two girls smiled good evening.

They love me, he thought, taking off his boots and hanging up his coat; I'm not like their English-speaking bosses.

I love myself, he thought with amazement even while conducting a drill on word order. I love myself for tramping down Sherbrooke Street in zero weather just to help them with noun clauses. I love myself standing behind this podium and showing Gilles Carrier and Claude Veilleux the difference between the past continuous and the simple past; or the sultry Armenian girl with the bewitching half-glasses that "put on" is not the same as "take on"; or telling the dashing Mr. Miguel Mayor, late of Madrid, that simple futurity can be expressed in four different ways, at least.

This is what mastery is like, he thought. Being superb in one's chosen field, not merely in one's mother tongue. A respected performer in the lecture halls of the major universities, equipped by twenty years' research in the remotest libraries, and slowly giving it back to those who must have it. Dishing it out suavely, even wittily. Being a legend. Being loved and a little feared.

"Yes, Mrs. David?"

A *sabra*: freckled, reddish hair, looking like a British model, speaks with a nifty British accent, and loves me.

"No," he smiled, *"I were* is not correct except in the present subjunctive, which you haven't studied yet."

The first hour's bell rang. In the halls of McGill they broke into the usual groups. French Canadians and South Americans into two large circles, then the Greeks, Germans, Spanish, and French into smaller groups. The patterns interested Dyer. Madrid Spaniards and Parisian French always spoke English with their New World co-linguals. The Middle Europeans spoke German together, not Russian, preferring one occupier to the other. Two Israeli men went off alone. Dyer decided to join them for the break.

Not *sabras,* Dyer concluded, not like Mrs. David. The shorter one, dark and wavy-haired, held his cigarette like a violin bow. The other, Mr. Weinrot, was tall and pot-bellied, with a ruddy face and thick stubby fingers. Something about him suggested truck-driving, perhaps of beer, maybe in Germany. Neither one, he decided, could supply the name of a good Israeli restaurant.

"This is really hard, you know?" said Weinrot.

"Why?"

"I think it's because I'm not speaking much of English at my job."

"French?" asked Dyer.

"French? Pah! All the time Hebrew, sometimes German, sometimes little Polish. Crazy thing, eh? How long you think they let me speak Hebrew if I'm working in America?"

"Depends on where you're working," he said.

"Hell, I'm working for the Canadian government, what you think? Plant I work in — I'm engineer, see — makes boilers for the turbines going up North. Look. When I'm leaving Israel I go first to Italy. Right away-bamm I'm working in Italy I'm speaking Italian like a native. Passing for a native."

"A native Jew," said his dark-haired friend.

"Listen to him. So in Rome they think I'm from Tyrol — that's still native, eh? So I speak Russian and German and Italian like a Jew. My Hebrew is bad, I admit it, but it's a lousy language anyway. Nobody likes it. French I understand but English I'm talking like a bum. Arabic I know five dialects. Danish fluent. So what's the matter I can't learn English?"

"It'll come, don't worry," Dyer smiled. *Don't worry, my son;* he wanted to pat him on the arm. "Anyway, that's what makes Canada so appealing. Here they don't force you."

"What's this *appealing*? Means nice? Look, my friend, keep it, eh? Two years in a country I don't learn the language means it isn't a country."

"Come on," said Dyer. "Neither does forcing you."

"Let me tell you a story why I come to Canada. Then you tell me if I was wrong, O.K.?"

"Certainly," said Dyer, flattered.

In Italy, Weinrot told him, he had lost his job to a Communist union. He left Italy for Denmark and opened up an Israeli restaurant with five other friends. Then the six Israelis decided to rent a bigger apartment downtown near the restaurant. They found a perfect nine-room place for two thousand kroner a month, not bad shared six ways. Next day the landlord told them the deal was off. "You tell me why," Weinrot demanded.

No Jews? Dyer wondered. "He wanted more rent," he finally said.

"More — you kidding? More we expected. *Less* we didn't expect. A couple with eight kids is showing up after we're gone and the law in Denmark says a man has a right to a room for each kid plus a hundred kroner knocked off the rent for each kid. What you think of that? So a guy who comes in *after* us gets a nine-room place for a thousand kroner *less*. Law says no way a bachelor can get a place ahead of a family, and bachelors pay twice as much."

Dyer waited, then asked, "So?"

"So, I make up my mind the world is full of communismus, just like Israel. So I take out applications next day for Australia, South Africa, U.S.A., and Canada. Canada says come right away, so I go. Should have waited for South Africa."

"How could you?" Dyer cried. "What's wrong with you anyway? South Africa is fascist. Australia is racist."

The bell rang, and the Israelis, with Dyer, began walking to the room.

"What I was wondering, then," said Mr. Weinrot, ignoring Dyer's outburst, "was if my English is good enough to be working in the United States. You're American, aren't you?"

It was a question Dyer had often avoided in Europe, but had rarely been asked in Montreal. "Yes," he admitted, "your English is probably good enough for the States or South Africa, whichever one wants you first."

He hurried ahead to the room, feeling that he had let Montreal down. He wanted to turn and shout to Weinrot and to all the others that Montreal was the greatest city on the continent, if only they knew it as well as he did. If they'd just break out of their little ghettos.

At the door, the Armenian girl with the half-glasses caught his arm. She was standing with Mrs. David and Miss Parizeau, a jolly French-Canadian girl that Dyer had been thinking of asking out.

"Please, sir," she said, looking at him over the tops of her tiny glasses, "what I was asking earlier — *put on* — I heard on the television. A man said *You are putting me on* and everybody laughed. I think it was supposed to be funny but *put on* we learned means get dressed, no?"

"Ah — *don't put me on,*" Dyer laughed.

"I yaven't erd it neither," said Miss Parizeau.

"To put some*body* on means to make a fool of him. To put some*thing* on is to wear it. O.K.?" He gave examples.

"Ah, now I know," said Miss Parizeau. "Like bull-shitting somebody. Is it the same?"

"Ah, yes," he said, smiling. French Canadians were like children learning the language. "Your example isn't considered polite. 'Put on' is very common now in the States."

"Then maybe," said Miss Parizeau, "we'll ave it ere in twenty years." The Armenian giggled.

"No — I've heard it here just as often," Dyer protested, but the girls had already entered the room.

He began the second hour with a smile which slowly soured as he thought of the Israelis. America's anti-communism was bad enough, but it was worse hearing it echoed by immigrants, by Jews, here in Montreal. Wasn't there a psychological type who chose Canada over South Africa? Or was it just a matter of visas and slow adjustment? Did Johannesburg lose its Greeks, and Melbourne its Italians, the way Dyer's students were always leaving Montreal?

And after class when Dyer was again feeling content and thinking of approaching one of the Israelis for a restaurant tip, there came the flood of small requests: should Mrs. Papadopoulos go into a more advanced course; could Mr. Perez miss a week for an interview in Toronto; could Mr. Giguère, who spoke English perfectly, have a harder book; Mr. Côté an easier one?

Then as he packed his briefcase in the empty room, Miguel Mayor, the vain and impeccable Spaniard, came forward from the hallway.

"Sir," he began, walking stiffly, ready to bow or salute. He wore a loud, gray checkered sportscoat this evening, blue shirt, and matching ascot-handkerchief, slightly mauve. He must have shaved just before class, Dyer noticed, for two fresh daubs of antiseptic cream stood out on his jaw, just under his earlobe. He stepped closer. "Sir?"

"What's on your mind, then?"

"Please — have you the time to look on a letter for me?"

He laid the letter on the podium.

"Look *over* a letter," said Dyer. "What is it for?"

"I have applied," he began, stopping to emphasize the present perfect construction, "for a job in Cleveland, Ohio, and I want to know if my letter will be good. Will an American, I mean — "

"Why are you going there?"

"It is a good job."

"But Cleveland — "

"They have a blackman mayor, I have read. But the job is not in Cleveland."

"Let me see it."

Most honourable Sir: I humbly beg consideration for a position in your grand company . . .

"Who are you writing this to?"

"The president," said Miguel Mayor.

I am once a student of Dr. Ramiro Gutierrez of the Hydraulic Institute of Sevilla, Spain . . .

"Does the president know this Ramiro Gutierrez?"

"Oh, everybody is knowing him," Miguel Mayor assured, "he is the most famous expert in all Spain."

"Did he recommend this company to you?"

"No — I have said in my letter, if you look — "

An ancient student of Dr. Gutierrez, Salvador del Este, is actually a boiler expert who is being employed like supervisor is formerly a friend of mine . . .

"Is he still your friend?"

Whenever you say come to my city Miguel Mayor for talking I will be coming. I am working in Montreal since two years and am now wanting more money than I am getting here now . . .

"Well . . . " Dyer sighed.

"Sir — what I want from you is knowing in good English how to interview me by this man. The letters in Spanish are not the same to English ones, you know?"

I remain humbly at your orders . . .

"Why do you want to leave Montreal?"

"It's time for a change."

"Have you ever been to Cleveland?"

"I am one summer in California. Very beautiful there and hot like my country. Montreal is big port like Barcelona. Everybody mixed together and having no money. It is just a place to land, no?"

"Montreal? Don't be silly."

"I thought I come here and learn good English but where I work I get by in Spanish and French. It's hard, you know?" he smiled. Then he took a few steps back and gave his cuffs a gentle tug, exposing a set of jade cuff links.

Dyer looked at the letter again and calculated how long he would be correcting it, then up at his student. How old is he? My age? Thirty? Is he married? Where do the Spanish live in Montreal? He looks so prosperous, so confident, like a male model off a page of *Playboy*. For an instant Dyer felt that his student was mocking him, somehow pitting his astounding confidence and wardrobe, sharp chin, and matador's bearing against Dyer's command of English and mastery of the side streets, bistros, and ethnic restaurants. Mayor's letter was painful, yet he remained somehow competent. He would pass his interview, if he got one. What would he care about America, and the odiousness he'd soon be supporting? It was as though a superstructure of exploitation had been revealed, and Dyer felt himself abused by the very people he wanted so much to help. It had to end someplace.

He scratched out the second "humbly" from the letter, then folded the sheet of foolscap. "Get it typed right away," he said. "Good luck."

"Thank you, sir," said his student, with a bow. Dyer watched the letter disappear in the inner pocket of the checkered sportscoat. Then the folding of the cashmere scarf, the draping of the camel's-hair coat about the shoulders, the easing of the fur hat down to the rims of his ears. The meticulous filling of the pigskin gloves. Mayor's patent leather galoshes glistened.

"Good evening, sir," he said.

"*Buenas noches,*" Dyer replied.

He hurried now, back down Sherbrooke Street to his daytime office where he could deposit his books. Montreal on a winter night was still mysterious, still magical. Snow blurred the arc lights. The wind was dying. Every second car was now a taxi, crowned with an orange crescent. Slushy curbs had hardened. The window of Holt Renfrew's was still attractive. The legless dummies invited a final stare. He stood longer than he had earlier, in front of the sporty mannequin with a burgundy waistcoat, the mauve and blue ensemble, the jade cuff links.

Good evening, sir, he could almost hear. The ascot, the shirt, the complete outfit, had leaped off the back of Miguel Mayor. He pictured how he must have entered the store with three hundred dollars and a prepared speech, and walked out again with everything off the torso's back.

I want that.

What, sir?

That.

The coat, sir?

Yes.

Very well, sir.

And *that.*

Which, sir?

All that.

"Absurd man!" Dyer whispered. There had been a moment of fear, as though the naked body would leap from the window, and legless, chase him down Sherbrooke Street. But the moment was passing. Dyer realized now that it was comic, even touching. Miguel Mayor had simply tried too hard, too fast, and it would be good for him to stay in Montreal until he deserved those clothes, that touching vanity and confidence. With one last look at the window, he turned sharply, before the clothes could speak again.

METAPHOR AND NATIONALITY
Allan Smith

Canada and the United States have been peopled by
immigrants. The experience that these immigrants have
undergone, and the character of the society they have helped
to form, has been described metaphorically in both countries.
One speaks of the American melting pot and the Canadian
mosaic. Each of these metaphors carries a double burden. Each
is supposed to symbolize the actual nature of the society to
which it is applied, and each is held to represent the ideal
form which that society is attempting to realize.

The melting-pot metaphor conjures up a picture of peoples
of diverse origins being fused in the crucible of a new
environment into a group of wholly new beings. Each of these
beings has severed his ties with the Old World, and each has
been regenerated by his new environment. Each has become,
in Crèvecoeur's classic phrase, a new man. This theme has
been one of endless fascination for Americans. They have
expended much time and energy elaborating the image of
America as a New World, a garden, a virgin land, free from
the corrupt and corrupting influences of the Old World, and
capable of regenerating man. The American, and all men who
come to America, are transformed.

In Canada the idea of creating a new man has gained
nothing like the currency it has in the United States. Here the
controlling metaphor has been the mosaic, a grand design
consisting of many different elements, each of which retains its
own character and quality while simultaneously contributing
to the realization of the design as a whole. The objective is the
rendering of a composite figure, not the creation of one that is
wholly new. The elements of which this composite figure, this
new nation, consists will be juxtaposed in such a way as to
create a new nationality, one which rests not upon a common
culture, but upon its capacity to serve and protect the
interests, cultural and otherwise, of its component parts. The
essence of this new nationality will be found in the nature of
the relationship these different elements bear to one another,

and not in the fact that there will cease to be different elements. There will need to be a consensus in this national state. It will, however, be a consensus which derives not so much from a shared culture or shared values as from the belief by all its peoples that their best interests are being served by continuing association in a common political framework.

Each of these metaphors idealizes the society to which it refers, and it idealizes the experience of the immigrant who has come to that society. Immigrants to the United States have often retained, and have often been encouraged to retain, some measure of their ethnic consciousness. . . .

To the extent that the immigrant to America has, however, been required to divest himself of his ethnic identity, he has not become a wholly new man. He and his fellows have not been melted down and then recast in an entirely new mould. They have become, instead, Americanized Englishmen. The dominant social type in the United States is an Anglo-Saxon type, and it is to this type that immigrants have been expected to assimilate. The American becomes, then, not a new man, but a modification of one who is old and familiar.

And so the term "anglo-conformity" has been held to describe more accurately than does the melting-pot metaphor what happens to the immigrant who comes to the United States.

Finally, while the immigrant to the United States might be assimilated to the prevailing culture and value system, he is not always assimilated into the agencies and institutions that operate society. His assimilation is behavioural, but not structural. It is not total, and here too, the melting-pot metaphor breaks down.

The mosaic concept is also an idealization of reality. A greater degree of behavioural assimilation has taken place in Canada than that concept would appear to allow for. The majority of second generation German-Canadians, Icelandic-Canadians, and even Ukrainian-Canadians speak English and not their parents' native tongue. Their Old World culture, when it is retained, is regarded as something to be brought out and dusted off, rather self-consciously, on special national occasions. It does not form a central part of Canada's cultural life, and when it is brought to the attention of Canadians at large, the tendency is to regard it as an imported exotic.

The mosaic further implies a social situation in which members of different ethnic communities are able to retain their ethnic identity, and yet participate to the full in the national life. Here, also, the metaphor fails to represent the reality. Positions of power, influence, and prestige have tended to go to Canadians of British descent, and continuing emphasis on ethnic origins has been judged likely to perpetuate this state of affairs.

Finally, a state dedicated to the proposition that all cultural groups within it have an inalienable right to flourish would be a state in which, ideally, brokerage politics would have no place. Representatives of each cultural group would know that their special interests would be looked after, and they would not, therefore, find it necessary to solicit special favours. The national interest would not demand constant adjustment of the claims of rival groups. And precisely because the interests of each group would, automatically as it were, be served, politicians would have nothing to gain by manoeuvring for the support of these groups. But this clearly is not the situation. Politicians who, as André Siegfried wrote at the beginning of the century, found it necessary to "exert themselves . . . to prevent the formation of homogeneous parties, divided according to creed or race or class" have noticed no changes in what is required of them. The different groups still feel it necessary to promote their interests, and those interests must still be reconciled with one another. It remains an essential part of politics in Canada to adjust the claims of different groups and interests and to insure as nearly as possible that none shall have undue influence and that the state shall not fragment along ethnic lines. The existence of the politician as broker indicates, not the presence of a fully functioning cultural mosaic, but its absence.

SUMMER ACRES
Anne Wilkinson

I

These acres breathe my family,
Holiday with seventy summers' history.
My blood lives here,
Sunned and veined three generations red
Before my bones were formed.

My eyes are wired to the willow
That wept for my father,
My heart is boughed by the cedar
That covers with green limbs the bones of my children,
My hands are white with a daisy, sired
By the self same flower my grandfather loved;

My ears are tied to the tattle of water
That echoes the vows of ancestral lovers,
My skin is washed by a lather of waves
That bathed the blond bodies of uncles and aunts
And curled on the long flaxen hair of my mother;

My feet step soft on descendants of grass
That was barely brushed
By the wary boots of a hummingbird woman,
The Great Great Grandmother
Of my mid-century children.

II

September born, reared in the sunset hour,
I was the child of old men heavy with honor;
I mourned the half-mast time of their death and sorrowed
A season for leaves, shaking their scarlet flags
From green virility of trees.

As ears spring cartilaged from skulls
So my ears spring from the sound of water
And the whine of autumn in the family tree.
How tired, how tall grow the trees
Where the trees and the family are temples
Whose columns will tumble, leaf over root to their ruin.

Here, in my body's home my heart dyes red
The last hard maple in their acres.
Where birch and elm and willow turn,
Gently bred, to gold against the conifers,
I hail my fathers, sing their blood to the leaf.

GREAT-AUNT REBECCA
Elizabeth Brewster

I remember my mother's Aunt Rebecca
Who remembered very well Confederation
And what a time of mourning it was.
She remembered the days before the railway,
And how when the first train came through
Everybody got on and visited it,
Scraping off their shoes first
So as not to dirty the carriage.
She remembered the remoteness, the long walks between
    neighbours.
Her own mother had died young, in childbirth,
But she had lived till her eighties,
Had borne eleven children,
Managed to raise nine of them,
In spite of scarlet fever.
She had clothed them with the work of her own fingers,
Wool from her own sheep, spun at home,
Woven at home, sewed at home
Without benefit of machine.
She had fed them with pancakes and salt pork
And cakes sweetened with maple sugar.
She had taught them one by one to memorize
"The chief end of man is to know God",
And she had also taught them to make porridge
And the right way of lighting a wood fire,
Had told the boys to be kind and courageous
And the girls never to raise their voices
Or argue with their husbands.

I remember her as an old woman,
Rheumatic, with folded hands,
In a rocking chair in a corner of the living room,
Bullied (for her own good) by one of her daughters.
She marveled a little, gently and politely,
At radios, cars, telephones;

But really they were not as present to her
As the world of her prime, the farmhouse
In the midst of woods, the hayfields
Where her husband and the boys swung their scythes
Through the burning afternoon, until she called for supper.

For me also, the visiting child, she made that world more real
Than the present could be. I too
Wished to be a pioneer,
To walk on snowshoes through remote pastures,
To live away from settlements an independent life
With a few loved people only; to be like Aunt Rebecca,
Soft as silk and tough as that thin wire
They use for snaring rabbits.

ANCIENT LINEAGE
Morley Callaghan

The young man from the Historical Club with a green
magazine under his arm got off the train at Clintonville. It
was getting dark but the station lights were not lit. He
hurried along the platform and jumped down on the sloping
cinder path to the sidewalk.

Trees were on the lawns alongside the walk, branches
drooping low, leaves scraping occasionally against the young
man's straw hat. He saw a cluster of lights, bluish-white in
the dusk across a river, many lights for a small town. He
crossed the lift-lock bridge and turned on to the main street.
A hotel was at the corner.

At the desk a bald-headed man in a blue shirt, the sleeves
rolled up, looked critically at the young man while he
registered. "All right, Mr. Flaherty," he said, inspecting the
signature carefully.

"Do you know many people around here?" Mr. Flaherty
asked.

"Just about everybody."

"The Rowers?"

"The old lady?"

"Yeah, an old lady."

"Sure, Mrs. Anna Rower. Around the corner to the left,
then turn to the right on the first street, the house opposite
the Presbyterian church on the hill."

"An old family," suggested the young man.

"An old-timer all right." The hotel man made it clear by a
twitching of his lips that he was a part of the new town,
canal, water power, and factories.

Mr. Flaherty sauntered out and turned to the left. It was
dark and the street had the silence of small towns in the
evening. Turning a corner he heard girls giggling in a
doorway. He looked at the church on the hill, the steeple dark
against the sky. He had forgotten whether the man had said
beside the church or across the road, but could not make up
his mind to ask the fellow who was watering the wide church
lawn. No lights in the shuttered windows of the rough-cast
house beside the church. He came down the hill and had to

yell three times at the man because the water swished strongly against the grass.

"All right, thanks. Right across the road," Mr. Flaherty repeated.

Tall trees screened the square brick house. Looking along the hall to a lighted room, Mr. Flaherty saw an old lady standing at a sideboard. "She's in all right," he thought, rapping on the screen door. A large woman of about forty, dressed in blue skirt and blue waist, came down the stairs. She did not open the screen door.

"Could I speak to Mrs. Anna Rower?"

"I'm Miss Hilda Rower."

"I'm from the University Historical Club."

"What did you want to see Mother for?"

Mr. Flaherty did not like talking through the screen door. "I wanted to talk to her," he said firmly.

"Well, maybe you'd better come in."

He stood in the hall while the large woman lit the gas in the front room. The gas flared up, popped, showing fat hips and heavy lines on her face. Mr. Flaherty, disappointed, watched her swaying down the hall to get her mother. He carefully inspected the front room, the framed photographs of dead Conservative politicians, the group of military men hanging over the old-fashioned piano, the faded greenish wallpaper, and the settee in the corner.

An old woman with a knot of white hair and good eyes came into the room, walking erectly. "This is the young man who wanted to see you, Mother," Miss Hilda Rower said. They all sat down. Mr. Flaherty explained he wanted to get some information concerning the Rower genealogical tree for the next meeting of his society. The Rowers, he knew, were a pioneer family in the district, and descended from William the Conqueror, he had heard.

The old lady laughed thinly, swaying from side to side. "It's true enough, but I don't know who told you. My father was Daniel Rower, who came to Ontario from Cornwall in 1830."

Miss Hilda Rower interrupted. "Wait, Mother, you may not want to tell about it." Brusque and businesslike, she turned to the young man. "You want to see the family tree, I suppose."

"Oh, yes."

"My father was a military settler here," the old lady said.

"I don't know but what we might be able to give you some notes," Miss Hilda spoke generously.

"Thanks awfully, if you will."

"Of course you're prepared to pay something if you're going to print it," she added, smugly adjusting her big body in the chair.

Mr. Flaherty got red in the face; of course he understood, but to tell the truth he had merely wanted to chat with Mrs. Rower. Now he knew definitely he did not like the heavy nose and unsentimental assertiveness of the lower lip of this big woman with the wide shoulders. He couldn't stop looking at her thick ankles. Rocking back and forth in the chair she was primly conscious of lineal superiority; a proud unmarried woman, surely she could handle a young man, half-closing her eyes, a young man from the University indeed. "I don't want to talk to her about the University," he thought.

Old Mrs. Rower went into the next room and returned with a framed genealogical tree of the house of Rower. She handed it graciously to Mr. Flaherty, who read, "The descent of the family of Rower, from William the Conqueror, from Malcolm 1st, and from the Capets, Kings of France." It bore the *imprimatur* of the College of Arms, 1838.

"It's wonderful to think you have this," Mr. Flaherty said, smiling at Miss Hilda, who watched him suspiciously.

"A brother of mine had it all looked up," old Mrs. Rower said.

"You don't want to write about that," Miss Hilda said, crossing her ankles. The ankles looked much thicker crossed. "You just want to have a talk with Mother."

"That's it," Mr. Flaherty smiled agreeably.

"We may write it up ourselves some day." Her heavy chin dipped down and rose again.

"Sure, why not?"

"But there's no harm in you talking to Mother if you want to, I guess."

"You could write a good story about that tree," Mr. Flaherty said, feeling his way.

"We may do it some day but it'll take time," she smiled complacently at her mother, who mildly agreed.

Mr. Flaherty talked pleasantly to this woman, who was so determined he would not learn anything about the family tree without paying for it. He tried talking about the city, then tactfully asked old Mrs. Rower what she remembered of the Clintonville of seventy years ago. The old lady talked willingly, excited a little. She went into the next room to get a book of clippings. "My father, Captain Rower, got a grant of land from the Crown and cleared it," she said, talking over her shoulder. "A little way up the Trent River. Clintonville was a small military settlement then . . . "

"Oh, Mother, he doesn't want to know all about that," Miss Hilda said impatiently.

"It's very interesting indeed."

The old woman said nervously, "My dear, what difference does it make? You wrote it all up for the evening at the church."

"So I did too," she hesitated, thinking the young man ought to see how well it was written. "I have an extra copy." She looked at him thoughtfully. He smiled. She got up and went upstairs.

The young man talked very rapidly to the old lady and took many notes.

Miss Rower returned. "Would you like to see it?" She handed Mr. Flaherty a small gray booklet. Looking quickly through it, he saw it contained valuable information about the district.

"The writing is simply splendid. You must have done a lot of work on it."

"I worked hard on it," she said, pleased and more willing to talk.

"Is this an extra copy?"

"Yes, it's an extra copy."

"I suppose I might keep it," he said diffidently.

She looked at him steadily. "Well . . . I'll have to charge you twenty-five cents."

"Sure, sure, of course, that's fine." He blushed.

"Just what it costs to get them out," the old lady explained apologetically.

"Can you change a dollar?" He fumbled in his pocket, pulling the dollar out slowly.

They could not change it but Miss Rower would be pleased to go down to the corner grocery store. Mr. Flaherty protested. No trouble, he would go. She insisted on asking the next-door neighbour to change it. She went across the room, the dollar in hand.

Mr. Flaherty chatted with the nice old lady and carefully examined the family tree, and wrote quickly in a small book till the screen door banged, the curtains parted, and Miss Hilda Rower came into the room. He wanted to smirk, watching her walking heavily, so conscious of her ancient lineage, a virginal mincing sway to her large hips, seventy-five cents' change held loosely in drooping fingers.

"Thank you," he said, pocketing the change, pretending his work was over. Sitting back in the chair, he praised the way Miss Rower had written the history of the neighbourhood, and suggested she might write a splendid story of the family tree, if she had the material, of course.

"I've got the material, all right," she said, trying to get comfortable again. How would Mr. Flaherty arrange it and where should she try to sell it? The old lady was dozing in the rocking-chair. Miss Rower began to talk rather nervously about her material. She talked of the last title in the family and the Sir Richard who had been at the court of Queen Elizabeth.

Mr. Flaherty chimed in gaily, "I suppose you know the O'Flahertys were kings in Ireland, eh?"

She said vaguely, "I daresay, I daresay," conscious only of an interruption to the flow of her thoughts. She went on talking with hurried eagerness, all the fine talk about her ancestors bringing her peculiar satisfaction. A soft light came into her eyes and her lips were moist.

Mr. Flaherty started to rub his cheek, and looked at her big legs, and felt restive, and then embarrassed, watching her closely, her firm lower lip hanging loosely. She was talking slowly, lazily, relaxing in her chair, a warm fluid oozing through her veins, exhausting but satisfying her.

He was uncomfortable. She was liking it too much. He did not know what to do. There was something immodest about it. She was close to forty, her big body relaxed in the chair. He looked at his watch and suggested he would be going. She stretched her legs graciously, pouting, inviting him to stay a while longer, but he was standing up, tucking his magazine under his arm. The old lady was still dozing. "I'm so comfortable," Miss Rower said, "I hate to move."

The mother woke up and shook hands with Mr. Flaherty. Miss Rower got up to say good-bye charmingly.

Halfway down the path Mr. Flaherty turned. She was standing in the doorway, partly shadowed by the tall trees, bright moonlight filtering through the leaves touching soft lines on her face and dark hair.

He went down the hill to the hotel, unconsciously walking with a careless easy stride, wondering at the change that had come over the heavy, strong woman. He thought of taking a walk along the river in the moonlight, the river on which old Captain Rower had drilled troops on the ice in the winter of 1837 to fight the rebels. Then he thought of having a western sandwich in the café across the road from the hotel. That big woman in her own way had been hot stuff.

In the hotel he asked to be called early so he could get the first train to the city. For a long time he lay awake in the fresh, cool bed, the figure of the woman, whose ancient lineage had taken the place of a lover in her life, drifting into his thoughts and becoming important while he watched on the wall the pale moonlight that had softened the lines of her face, and wondered if it was still shining on her bed, and on her throat, and on her contented, lazily relaxed body.

QUESTIONS ON THE THEME:
The Immigrant Experience

1. In "The Fever of Immigration" Susanna Moodie gives three reasons for immigration to Canada: "duty, necessity, and love of independence". How are these three motives illustrated or implied in the poems "Emigrants", "Young Canada", and "Calgary Station", and in the short stories "The Decision" and "The Well of Dunrea"?

2. It is understandable that emigrants feel ambivalent about leaving their native country. They want both to leave and to stay. How do the following selections show this twofold pull: "The Fever of Immigration", "Calgary Station", and "Christie's First Tale of Piper Gunn"?

3. Another ambivalence is felt by those who are unwilling to give up the ideals of the old society they have left behind, and who place their pride in the accomplishments of their native land. In the following selections, what problems does this pride create: "Bambinger", "Back Door", "A Class of New Canadians", "Ancient Lineage", and "Colonial Set"?

4. The passage from old country to new marks immigrants' minds with confusion and elation which writers try to portray through their own imaginations. How do the writers of "Further Arrivals", "Calgary Station", and "Emigrants" imagine their voyagers' reactions?

5. Newcomers to unsettled lands have been compared to Adam and Eve in the Garden of Eden. What parallels do you see? Referring to "The Well of Dunrea" and "A Class of New Canadians", explore the idea of innocence and guilt in the new Canadian, as well as the roles of their God-like supervisors, Mr. Roy and Mr. Dyer.
   How is the idea of the Promised Land shown in "The Decision", "Back Door", and "In the Wilderness"?
   What is the importance of the land itself in "The Well of Dunrea" and "All the Spikes But the Last"?

6. People stay together in groups because they are afraid of the unfamiliar, or because they are loyal to the group. Early arrivals feel superior to those who come along later. With reference to *The Immigrant Experience*, examine these three statements for which the euphemism is "cultural solidarity".

7. Writers about immigrants are sometimes accused of creating racial or cultural stereotypes. Can you find any examples of stereotypes in this anthology? Why do authors use stereotypes? In your discussion, refer to Allan Smith's essay in which he discusses whether or not we have a true "mosaic" in Canada.

8. It is the children of immigrants who make the strongest effort to shake off the old world and become part of the new. How is their assimilation described in "Bambinger", "Back Door", "Calgary Station", and "Metaphor and Nationality"? What attitude toward getting ahead, or "making it", is shown by adults in "A Class of New Canadians" and "A Wedding in Toronto"?

9. There are several ways to define a myth. Sometimes the myth is about a person who seems "larger than life". Do Great-Aunt Rebecca and the Man from Manitoba ("The Decision") have the qualities of mythical heroes?

Sometimes myths involve real historical figures. How do Margaret Laurence and Al Purdy mythologize the people in their writings?

Sometimes, remarkable ancestries have the properties of myths; their telling can have an effect on us. What is the effect of the story on the teller or the listener in "Ancient Lineage" and "Great-Aunt Rebecca"?

10. Most genuine humour about immigrants is gentle humour. Can you suggest why? Consider the following questions about how authors treated subjects that might have been considered laughable:

Does Al Purdy mock the Doukhobors in "In the Wilderness"?

Is F. R. Scott's question to his friend E. J. Pratt a laughing matter?

Is Susanna Moodie overstating emigrants' expectations that sheep and oxen "will be ready roasted, and with knives and forks upon their backs" in order to make a joke?

What is the reason for Callaghan's ironical approach toward the character of Miss Rower?

Why do the creators of the confident immigrants *not* take their characters seriously, e.g., Bambinger and Mr. Dyer?

Why do authors imitate immigrant patterns of speech, e.g., in "Back Door", "Bambinger", "Christie's First Tale of Piper Gunn", and "A Class of New Canadians"?

BIBLIOGRAPHY

BIOGRAPHICAL INFORMATION

Carl F. Klinck, *A Literary History of Canada: Canadian Literature in English*, University of Toronto Press

Norah Story, *The Oxford Companion to Canadian History and Literature*, Oxford University Press

William Stewart Wallace, *The Macmillan Dictionary of Canadian Biography*, Macmillan of Canada

NOVELS

Frances Moore Brooke, *The History of Emily Montague*, New Canadian Library

Ralph Connor, *The Foreigner*, University of Toronto Press

Mazo de la Roche, *Jalna*, Macmillan of Canada

Sara Duncan, *The Imperialist*, New Canadian Library

Margaret Epp, *The Earth Is Round*, Christian Press, Winnipeg

Hugh Garner, *Cabbagetown*, McGraw-Hill

Frederick Philip Grove, *Fruits of the Earth, Master of the Mill, A Search for America, Settlers of the Marsh,* New Canadian Library

Henry Kreisel, *The Rich Man*, New Canadian Library

Margaret Laurence, *A Jest of God*, McClelland & Stewart; *The Stone Angel*, New Canadian Library

Vera Lysenko, *Yellow Boots*, Ryerson

John Marlyn, *Under the Ribs of Death*, Macmillan of Canada

Brian Moore, *The Luck of Ginger Coffey*, New Canadian Library

Martha Ostenso, *Wild Geese*, New Canadian Library

John Richardson, *Wacousta*, New Canadian Library

Mordecai Richler, *The Apprenticeship of Duddy Kravitz*, New Canadian Library

Laura G. Salverson, *The Viking Heart*, New Canadian Library

Robert Stead, *Grain*, New Canadian Library; *The Homesteaders*, University of Toronto Press

Rudy Wiebe, *Peace Shall Destroy Many*, New Canadian Library

Adele Wiseman, *The Sacrifice*, Macmillan of Canada

BIOGRAPHIES AND CHRONICLES

Willem de Gelder, *A Dutch Homesteader on the Prairies*, University of Toronto Press

Klaas de Jong, *Cauliflower Crown*, Western Producer

William Dunlop, *Tiger Dunlop's Upper Canada*, New Canadian
  Library
Elisabeth Gerrard, *We Came to Canada*, Longman Canada
Anna B. Jameson, *Winter Studies and Summer Rambles in Canada*,
  New Canadian Library
Jean Johnston, *Wilderness Women*, Peter Martin
Grant MacEwen, *John Ware's Cow Country*, Applied Art
Fredelle B. Maynard, *Raisins and Almonds*, PaperJacks
Susanna Moodie, *Roughing It in the Bush*, New Canadian Library
Audrey Morris, *The Gentle Pioneers*, PaperJacks
Barry Riddell, et al., *Minority Groups* (*Man in Society* series),
  Macmillan of Canada
Laura G. Salverson, *Confessions of an Immigrant's Daughter*, Reprint
  Society of Canada
Catherine Parr Traill, *The Backwoods of Canada, The Canadian
  Settler's Guide*, New Canadian Library

POETRY

Margaret Atwood, *The Journals of Susanna Moodie*, Oxford
  University Press
Al Purdy, *In Search of Owen Roblin*, McClelland & Stewart
David Sinclair (ed.), *Nineteenth-Century Poems*, New Canadian
  Library
J. Michael Yates (ed.), *Volvox*, Sono Nis Press

PLAYS

Bob Aaron, *et al.,* "Doukhobors", Playwrights' Co-op
Catherine Brickenden, "Zanorin" in *Canada On Stage*, Clarke,
  Irwin
J. B. Cowan, "Canuck", Rose, Cowan & Lotta
Mazo de la Roche, "Whiteoaks", Macmillan, London
Joan Forman, "Westward to Canaan", Holt, Rinehart & Winston of Canada
O. Kupchenko, "A Cold Winter and a Dead Spring", Alberta
  Dept. of Culture, Youth and Recreation, Edmonton
Audrey McKim, "New Horizons for Rolling Prairie" in *A
  Playette Quartet*, Friendship Press, N.Y.

Lister Sinclair, "The New Canada" in *A Play on Words and Other Radio Plays*, Dent (Canada); "The Blood Is Strong", Book Society of Canada

TAPES AND RECORDINGS
(Available from CBC Learning Systems; for an annotated catalogue, write to CBC Learning Systems, Box 500, Terminal A, Toronto, Ontario, M5W 1E6.)
Al Purdy's Ontario, 12" LP
The Bias of Culture (ages 12 to 15), 30 minutes, 882-4
Canada: Melting Pot or Mosaic, M. McKenna and R. Carlson, 30 minutes, 656
The Canadian Imagination, Northrop Frye, 30 minutes, 650
Cultivating the Differences, 30 minutes, 991
Immigrants to Power, David Rabinovitch, 60 minutes, 797L
Journals of Susanna Moodie, 12" LP
Last Spring They Came Over: The Short Stories of Morley Callaghan Introduced and Read by the Author, 30 minutes, 619
Myth and National Culture, one of a seven-part series, each 30 minutes, 91-7
The Texture of Mono Mills, 30 minutes, 865

FILMS, VIDEOTAPES, SLIDES
Antonio, NFB, 27 minutes (Note: For an annotated catalogue of NFB films, write to the nearest regional office of the National Film Board of Canada, or Information Canada.)
The Drylanders, NFB, feature length
Kurelek, NFB, 10 minutes
Paul Tomkowicz, Street Railway Switchman, NFB, 9 minutes
Twenty Million People, NFB, 25 minutes
The Visit, NFB, 27 minutes
Why Canada?, NFB, 28 minutes
The Apprenticeship of Duddy Kravitz, Paramount, feature length
Heritage, five films on Japan, Italy, Ireland, Germany, France, Xerox of Canada Ltd., 703 Don Mills Rd., Don Mills, Ontario, M3C 1S2, 60 minutes each

Journey Into Our Heritage, Jewish Historical Society, Room 403, 22 Donald St., Winnipeg, 16 mm, 30 minutes

Men in Sheepskin Coats (The Development of the Canadian West series), 28-minute videotape, available from:

Ontario Education Communication Authority, Canada Square, 2180 Yonge St., Toronto M4S 2C1

Access, Suite 400, Barnett House, 11010−142 St., Edmonton T5N 2R1

Société Radio Canada, P.O. Box 6000, Montreal 133, P.Q. (French translation)

Reflections of the Past, Ukrainian Cultural and Educational Centre, 184 Alexander Ave., Winnipeg R3C 2K3, feature length

Visual History Series, National Museum of Man, Ottawa, each 30 slides with text: "British Immigration to British North America, 1815-1860", "Immigration to Western Canada, 1896-1914", "Winnipeg, the Growth of a City"

57   67   77   87   97   08   18   28   38   THB   9   8   7   6   5   4   3   2   1